OECD
ECONOMIC
SURVEYS

1993-1994

NETHERLANDS

ORGANISATION FOR ECONOMIC CO-OPERATION AND DEVELOPMENT

ORGANISATION FOR ECONOMIC CO-OPERATION AND DEVELOPMENT

Pursuant to Article 1 of the Convention signed in Paris on 14th December 1960, and which came into force on 30th September 1961, the Organisation for Economic Co-operation and Development (OECD) shall promote policies designed:

- to achieve the highest sustainable economic growth and employment and a rising standard of living in Member countries, while maintaining financial stability, and thus to contribute to the development of the world economy;
- to contribute to sound economic expansion in Member as well as non-member countries in the process of economic development; and
- to contribute to the expansion of world trade on a multilateral, non-discriminatory basis in accordance with international obligations.

The original Member countries of the OECD are Austria, Belgium, Canada, Denmark, France, Germany, Greece, Iceland, Ireland, Italy, Luxembourg, the Netherlands, Norway, Portugal, Spain, Sweden, Switzerland, Turkey, the United Kingdom and the United States. The following countries became Members subsequently through accession at the dates indicated hereafter: Japan (28th April 1964), Finland (28th January 1969), Australia (7th June 1971), New Zealand (29th May 1973) and Mexico (18th May 1994). The Commission of the European Communities takes part in the work of the OECD (Article 13 of the OECD Convention).

3 2280 00497 9829

Publié également en français.

Table of contents

Tables

Diagrams

Text

BASIC STATISTICS OF THE NETHERLANDS

THE LAND

Area, 1992 (1 000 sq. km)	41.5	Major cities, 1st January 1993 (thousand inhabitants):	
Agricultural area (as a percentage of total)	64.2	Amsterdam	720
Forest (as a percentage of total)	8.0	Rotterdam	596
		The Hague	445

THE PEOPLE

Population, 1993 (thousands)	15 239	Employment, 1992 (thousands):	
Number of inhabitants per sq. km	449	Total	5 323
Net natural increase, 1993 (thousands)	67	Agriculture, fishing	260
		Industry	1 386
		Other activities	3 677

PRODUCTION

Gross domestic product, 1993		Origin of net domestic product	
(billion guilders)	573.4	at factor cost, 1993 (per cent):	
GDP per head (US$), 1993	20 265	Agriculture	3.6
Gross fixed investment:		Industry	22.6
Per cent of GDP, 1993	19.7	Construction	6.0
Per head (US$), 1993	3 983	Other	67.8

THE PUBLIC SECTOR

Public consumption, 1993 (% of GDP)	14.5	Composition of Parliament (No. of seats):	
Current receipts, 1993		Social-democrats	37
(% of GDP)	52.9	Christian-democrats	34
Current disbursement, 1993		Liberals (right)	31
(% of GDP)	53.5	Liberals (left)	24
		Other	24
		Total	150
		Last general election: May 1994	

FOREIGN TRADE

Exports of goods and services, 1992		Imports of goods and services, 1992	
(% of GDP)	52.3	(% of GDP)	47.8
Main exports, 1992		Main imports, 1992	
(% of total merchandise exports):		(% of total merchandise imports):	
Food	18.0	Food, beverages and tobacco	12.3
Energy	8.4	Energy	7.8
Chemicals	15.9	Manufactured goods except metal	9.4
Metals	6.2	Machinery and electrical equipment	22.4
Machinery and transport equipment	23.8	Transport equipment	9.2

THE CURRENCY

Monetary unit: Guilder		Currency units per US$,	
		average of daily figures:	
		Year 1993	1.86
		May 1994	1.86

Note: An international comparison of certain basic statistics is given in an annex table.

This Survey is based on the Secretariat's study prepared for the annual review of the Netherlands by the Economic and Development Review Committee. The Committee approved the Survey for publication on 13th June 1994.

•

The previous Survey of the Netherlands was issued in May 1993.

Introduction

The Dutch economy is emerging from a cyclical downturn which, contrary to fears entertained at the time of the previous EDRC examination of the Netherlands, has been shallow both compared with previous ones and with developments in neighbouring countries. This has largely reflected the structure of production and exports, with a relatively important share of agricultural products and services which are not very sensitive to cyclical variations. Exports have also been underpinned by a competitive pricing policy of Dutch firms. Hence, an improvement in the foreign balance more than offset a decline in total domestic demand last year, and the economy continued to grow, albeit at a very slow pace. Progress was recorded towards wage moderation, as agreed by the social partners, but unemployment rose steeply and non-employment edged-up further from already high levels. While economic growth is projected to accelerate this year and next, the recovery is unlikely to be sufficiently strong to have a significant impact on unemployment, although the rise in wages and prices may abate further.

The fundamental soundness of Dutch hard-currency policy centred around a close link between the guilder and the Deutschemark was evidenced again by last year's ERM crisis. Confidence in the guilder, if anything, strengthened and Dutch interest rates remained among the lowest in Europe. The Netherlands has also been more successful than most other European countries in reducing the public sector budget deficit. However, the public debt/GDP ratio is still not on a downward trend, as required to meet the Maastricht criteria. The "collective burden" (the share of taxes and social security contributions in Net National Income) remains one of the highest in the OECD area and is well above the ceiling set by the 1989 Coalition Agreement. Faced with weak activity, the Government decided to relax fiscal policy in 1994. On the structural side, several new measures have been taken, notably in the area of disability and competition policy. Nonetheless, progress has been slow and, on the whole, structural policy has been distinctly less successful than monetary policy and fiscal policy. The labour market and the welfare system have remained the major problems in an otherwise basically healthy economy. While the recent increase in unemployment may be largely cyclical, past experience suggests that without sufficient flexibility in the labour market, cyclical unemployment tends to become structural. Aware of the urgency of the situation, the Government has been considering a large number of measures to address the interrelated problems in the labour market and the social security system.

Part I briefly reviews the salient features of the downturn before considering recent trends and prospects. Part II first discusses monetary policy and monetary conditions; it then surveys efforts of the authorities to achieve the various goals of fiscal policy; finally, it presents a progress report on structural reforms, especially in the area of competition and competition policy. Part III deals with the labour market: the relentless increase in unemployment and non-employment; the many structural rigidities and social considerations which seem to be at the root of the problem; and the evolution of labour-market policy and new measures under consideration. Part IV gives a summary of the main findings and presents policy conclusions.

I. Recent trends and prospects: from a shallow downturn to a gradual recovery

Overview of the downturn

The recent downturn has been shallow, both compared with previous ones and with developments in the EC and especially in Germany. While in 1974-76 (marginally) and 1981-82 the economy actually contracted, in 1992-93 it slowed but continued to grow (Diagram 1, panel A); and while in the past the Dutch economy had closely followed the German one in its conjunctural upswings and downswings, this time the cycle has been considerably flatter in the Netherlands than in Germany (Diagram 2). One reason for the relatively good performance of the Dutch economy over the last couple of years is its pattern of specialisation, with a comparatively small share of manufacturing, and a large share of industrial food production and services which are less sensitive to cyclical variations than durable consumption and investment goods (Table 1). In particular, a salient feature of this cycle has been a sharp drop in the demand for cars: since the Netherlands has practically no automobile industry, its economy has suffered relatively little on this account. Also, private consumption has remained resilient, reflecting among other factors the healthy financial position of households and a sizeable wealth effect due to a strong recovery of bond and share prices as well as to an increase in real estate prices. These considerations, on balance, also suggest that the upturn is likely to be milder in the Netherlands than in surrounding countries.

In other respects, however, the effects of the downturn have been more pronounced. As Dutch exporters are largely price takers – especially in agriculture, the food industry and processing industries – they had to follow competitors and reduce prices markedly (Diagram 1, panel B). As a result, profit margins have been squeezed not only on exports but also on domestic sales. The capital

11

Diagram 1. **COMPARISON OF ECONOMIC DOWNTURNS**[1]
% changes

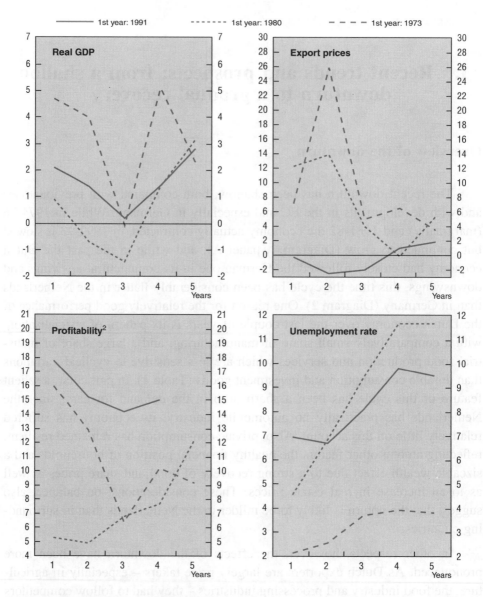

1. 1994 and 1995 observations are OECD Secretariat projections.
2. Share of capital in business GDP (excluding mining and housing).
Source: OECD Secretariat.

Diagram 2. INTERNATIONAL COMPARISON OF BUSINESS CYCLES

GDP, % changes

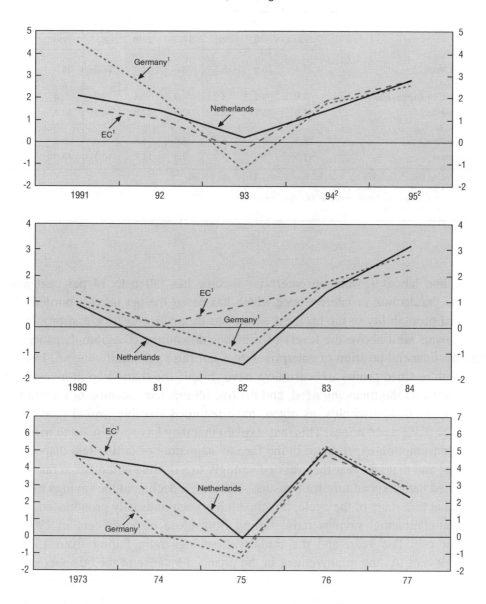

1. Before 1991, only western Germany, after 1991, total Germany.
2. OECD Secretariat projections.
Source: OECD Secretariat.

Table 1. **Structure of production**

Per cent of GDP

	Netherlands			Germany			EC[1]	
	1970	1980	1992	1970	1980	1992[2]	1980	1990
Manufacturing	24.4	16.9	18.3	38.4	32.4	28.7	26.2	23.6
of which:								
Food, beverages and tobacco	3.8	2.7	3.2	4.9	3.8	3.2	3.4	3.0
Private services[3]	41.6	46.7	52.6	32.3	37.8	44.3	40.3	46.4
of which:								
Transports	6.9	6.1	6.4	5.6	5.8	5.4	5.9	6.1
Government	11.1	13.0	9.9	9.3	11.7	10.3	13.0	12.6

1. Excluding United Kingdom for food, beverages and tobacco and Ireland.
2. Except for food and services: 1991.
3. Trade, restaurants and hotels, transport and other services.
Source: OECD Secretariat.

– *i.e.* non labour – share in enterprise income has fallen to 14 per cent and, despite the decline in interest rates which has eased the net interest burden, the level of profitability in the business sector has dropped. Nevertheless, profitability remains well above the levels of previous downturns (Diagram 1, panel C), and the financial position of enterprises does not raise particular concern. In fact, although retained profits and cash flow have shrunk, the sharp drop in investment has decreased the financing need, and the overall financial position of enterprises has improved. Households, as noted, have recorded sizeable capital gains as a result of rising asset prices. This may explain that they have continued to increase their consumption expenditure in the face of stagnating or falling real disposable income; and that last year they reacted strongly to a decline in mortgage rates and increased their expenditure for housing. Although a decline in the savings ratio is normal at this stage of the cycle, this time it has been unusually pronounced, with the non-contractual savings ratio[1] falling from close to 5 per cent in 1990 to 1.6 per cent last year, and the traditional savings ratio falling from 15.2 to 12.5 per cent. As the improvement in the financial balance of the business sector and the public sector more than offset the deterioration in the position of the household sector, the current-account surplus widened to nearly 3 per cent of GDP in 1993. This was in sharp contrast with developments in 1974-75 and 1981-82 when the current-account position was generally weaker. The impact of

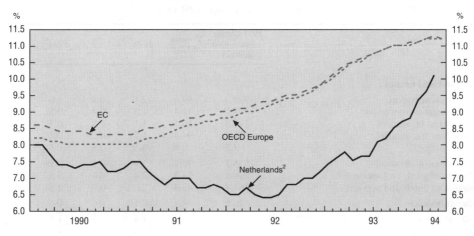

Diagram 3. **UNEMPLOYMENT RATE:[1] AN INTERNATIONAL COMPARISON**

1. Standardised rate.
2. 1993 and 1994 figures are OECD Secretariat estimates.
Source: OECD Secretariat.

this downturn on the labour market and unemployment has also been relatively strong (Diagram 1, panel D and Diagram 3), but more delayed than in other European countries. As discussed below, the Dutch unemployment rate continued to trend down in the early stages of the cycle and then rose steeply, as "labour hoarding" gave way to a "labour shake-out".

Demand and output

The economy slowed for the third year in a row in 1993, with real GDP growth falling from 1.4 per cent in 1992 to a mere ¼ per cent (Table 2). Growth was recorded only in the services sector, agriculture and the energy sector. Weak foreign demand and declining investment resulted in a contraction in industry and construction. Seen from the demand side, growth was entirely accounted for by an improvement in the foreign balance which outweighed a decline in total domestic demand. Underpinned by a competitive pricing policy and their relatively cyclical-insensitive composition, exports of goods and services, in volume,

15

Table 2. **Demand and output: recent trends and projections**

Annual percentage change, 1991 prices

	1991 Current prices billion guilders	Per cent of GDP	1992	1993	1994	1995
Demand and output						
Private consumption	323.0	59.6	2.1	0.8	1.0	2.0
Government consumption	77.9	14.4	1.3	−0.4	0.5	0.5
Gross fixed investment	110.8	20.5	1.1	−2.8	0.3	4.0
Final domestic demand	511.8	94.4	1.7	−0.2	0.8	2.2
Stockbuilding[1]	3.5	0.6	−0.3	−0.3	0.1	0.2
Total domestic demand	515.2	95.1	1.4	−0.5	0.9	2.4
Exports of goods and services	294.4	54.3	2.4	0.4	3.6	5.4
Imports of goods and services	267.8	49.4	2.6	−0.9	2.8	4.8
Foreign balance[1]	26.6	4.9	0.1	0.6	0.6	0.6
GDP at constant prices			1.4	0.2	1.4	2.8
GDP price deflator			2.5	1.6	2.0	2.1
GDP at current prices	541.9	100.0	3.9	1.8	3.5	5.0
Memorandum items:						
Private consumption deflator			3.0	2.1	2.1	2.0
Private compensation per employee			4.4	3.2	2.3	2.0
Total employment			2.0	0.8	−0.5	1.3
Unemployment rate			6.7	8.1	9.8	9.5
Breakdown of gross fixed investment						
Public sector	13.9	2.6	4.9	−1.1	7.1	3.5
Private sector residential	25.3	4.7	4.3	0.8	1.3	2.5
Private sector non-residential	71.6	13.2	−0.8	−4.4	−1.5	4.7
Net lending general government (per cent of GDP)			−3.5	−2.9	−3.9	−3.7
Household non-contractual saving ratio[2]			2.4	1.6	1.2	1.2
Short-term interest rate			9.4	7.0	5.0	4.3
Long-term interest rate			8.1	6.4	6.4	6.1
Current balance (per cent of GDP)			2.1	2.8	3.3	3.5

1. Contribution to growth of GDP.
2. Excluding net contributions (actual and imputed) to life insurance and pension schemes.
Source: OECD Secretariat estimates.

continued to increase, albeit at a very slow pace. On the other hand, imports, in volume, fell substantially as a result of sluggish domestic demand. However, these results must be regarded as somewhat tentative, as the measurement of trade flows has been hampered by the elimination of custom controls between EC countries following the introduction of the single market. Private consumption was the best performing component of domestic demand, although its growth rate more than halved, from 2.1 per cent in 1992 to 0.8 per cent. It dipped in the first quarter, mainly because of a sharp decline in car purchases but it rallied in the two subsequent quarters, before easing again in the final quarter. The drop in passenger car sales reached 20 per cent for the year as a whole, but to a significant extent this reflected stepped-up sales in late 1992, in anticipation of tax measures, and correspondingly weaker sales in early 1993. Allowing for this distorting factor, car sales declined by an estimated 10 per cent in 1993, broadly in line with the European average. Consumer durables which, as in other countries, typically show a more pronounced cycle than private consumption as a whole, contracted by 3 per cent – a relatively mild development compared with the experience of the early 1980s.

Gross fixed investment actually declined in 1993, for the first time since 1982 (Diagram 4, panel A). While public investment and residential investment changed little, the fall in business investment which had already started in 1992, accelerated to 4$\frac{1}{2}$ per cent. The average decline for OECD Europe was over 8 per cent, but excluding ships, airplanes and the energy sector, the decline in Dutch business investment also reached 8 per cent. As in most other European countries, the main reasons for this poor performance has been deteriorating sales prospects at home and abroad, depressed business confidence and declining capacity utilisation. However, compared with previous cyclical downturns the rate of capacity utilisation – at around 80 per cent – was not especially low in 1993 and it has rebounded significantly in the first quarter of 1994. While business investment does not seem to have been greatly affected by high real interest rates, it may have reacted more to the fall in profits. In fact, the long-standing good visual correlation between the share of profits (or conversely, of wages) in business sector GDP and net business investment (as a percentage of GDP) has continued during this downturn (Diagram 4, panel C). Investment has been weak in almost all sectors of the economy, except in the energy sector where it increased by nearly 35 per cent last year.[2] Firms have also reduced their stockbuilding, a development which has been broadly in line with previous cyclical downturns and that last year reduced GDP growth by 0.3 per cent.

Residential investment grew slightly last year. But this net result masked strongly divergent developments. While housing starts in the subsidised sector decreased by 19 per cent, those in the unsubsidised sector increased by 25 per

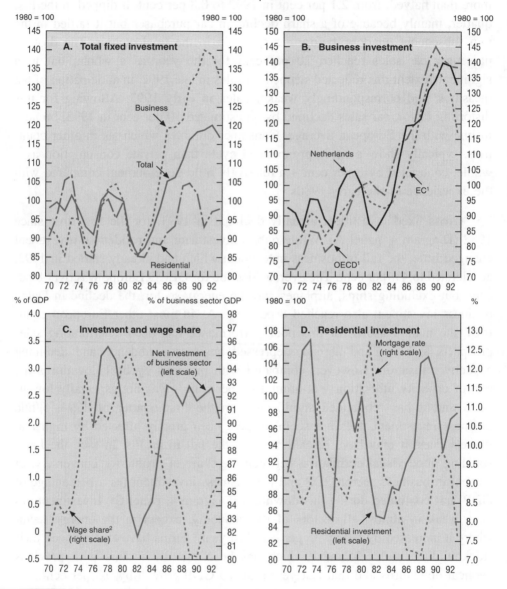

Diagram 4. **PRIVATE FIXED INVESTMENT**
At 1990 prices

A. Total fixed investment

Business

Total

Residential

B. Business investment

Netherlands

EC[1]

OECD[1]

C. Investment and wage share

Net investment
of business sector
(left scale)

Wage share[2]
(right scale)

D. Residential investment

Mortgage rate
(right scale)

Residential investment
(left scale)

1. Before 1991, only western Germany, after 1991, total Germany.
2. Business sector.
Sources: Central Bureau of Statistics, *National Accounts;* Central Planning Bureau submission and OECD, *Financial Statistics Monthly.*

18

cent. The buoyancy of the latter sector reflected primarily the decline in mortgage rates, the continuing rise in real rents, and the trend increase in the number of two-income-earner families (Diagram 4, panel D). In the subsidised sector building targets were not realised mainly because of administrative problems, such as finding appropriate locations and delays in town and country planning procedures. Overall, investment in new houses increased by 1.8 per cent but this was partly offset by a decline in investment in restoration.

Public investment declined somewhat, after a strong increase in 1992: as a proportion of GDP it fell below 3 per cent. It was undermined by problems in the implementation of government expenditure in this area. Public consumption also declined, albeit slightly, reflecting fiscal consolidation and continuing efforts to increase efficiency and cut costs. Employment in the public sector was stable (in full-time equivalents), in spite of "efficiency operations" (see Part II) and cuts in defence.

Costs and prices

Cost-price performance improved in 1993, following a couple years of fairly rapid increases in consumer prices and wages partly as a result of fiscal measures aimed at correcting structural budget imbalances. The deceleration has reflected several factors, including the conjunctural situation, a positive impact of fiscal measures and an agreement between the social partners to promote wage moderation.

The increase in wages slowed during 1993, as inflation declined, economic conditions worsened, and the impact of the central wage agreement between the social partners of November 1992 began to be felt. This agreement – the first since 1982 – included a wage freeze until March 1993 (or, more precisely, a postponement of major negotiations until March 1993) and a broad understanding that wage moderation would be extended beyond that date if economic conditions required it. This postponement enabled unions and employers to review and moderate their demands in the light of worsening conjunctural conditions and prospects. However, for 1993 on average, the rate of growth of collectively agreed wages still reached 3¼ per cent – compared with 4.4 per cent in 1992. As a small wage drift (¼ per cent) was offset by a reduction in social security contributions of employers, the growth in private compensation per employee in the private sector also amounted to 3¼ per cent – compared with 4.4 per cent in 1992. After accelerating for three years in a row, the increase in unit labour costs abated appreciably.

The authorities have actively encouraged wage moderation, taking various initiatives. The decision of the Government to freeze legal minimum wages and social benefits in nominal terms in 1993 may have contributed to restrain wage increases both in the private and the public sectors. The technical reason for the freeze (which was subsequently extended to 1994) was an expected dependency ratio[3] of 0.84 in 1993, above the reference level of 0.83. Also, following contractual wage settlements in 1992 judged as being too generous and fearing an actual increase in wages of more than 4 per cent in 1993, the Government seriously considered imposing a statutory wage freeze, a position which may have favourably affected the outcome of the November 1993 central wage agreement. This new agreement stated that there will be little or no room for nominal wage increases in 1994, but left it to negotiators at the decentralised level to implement this general guideline with flexibility.

Ongoing wage negotiations point to further wage moderation. Contractual wage increases for 1994 are known for around 75 per cent of employees in the market sector. The pay scale of these employees in set to rise by 1¾ per cent in annual terms. Most of these 1994 collective labour agreements had been concluded before the latest central agreement. Among those negotiated afterwards, in a few cases unions and employers' organisations have agreed on keeping nominal wages unchanged in 1994. Also, in the semi-public sector, the duration of some agreements has been prolonged from three to six months (with no increases in pay scales during this period). All considered, the authorities expect an average wage increase of around 2 per cent in 1994, or some 1¼ percentage points less than in 1993.

Inflation, measured by the CPI, decreased from 3.2 per cent in 1992 to 2.6 per cent in 1993, falling below inflation in Germany and in the average of partner countries (Diagram 5).[4] But underlying inflation – excluding food and energy prices – barely decelerated, and at 3.7 per cent was virtually the same as the EC average (3.8 per cent) and somewhat above the OECD average (3.1 per cent). To a significant extent, the better CPI inflation performance was due to the broad stabilisation of the price of medical services. Policy measures, which in 1991-92 had contributed to the acceleration of inflation, had a distinctly less

Diagram 5. **CONSUMER PRICE DEVELOPMENTS**

Change over corresponding period of previous year

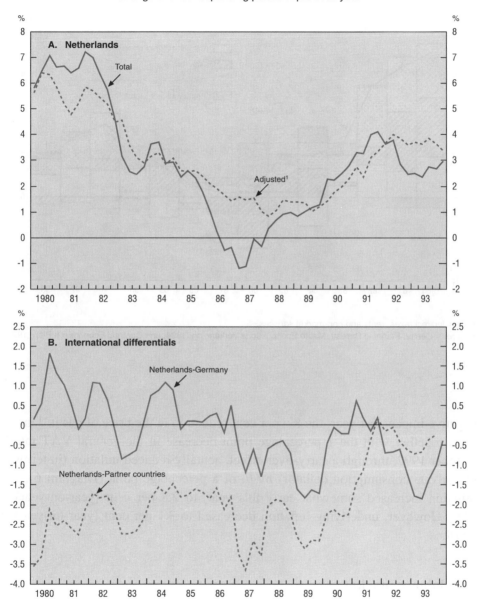

1. Excluding food and energy.
Source: OECD, *Main Economic Indicators* and estimates.

21

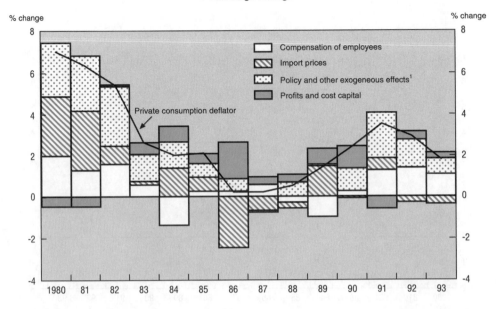

Diagram 6. **CONTRIBUTIONS TO THE PRIVATE CONSUMPTION DEFLATOR**
Percentage change

1. Gas, indirect taxes, rents and non-market services.
Sources: Central Planning Bureau, Macro Economische Verkenning, 1994, and Centraal Economisch Plan, 1994.

negative impact last year: the 8½ per cent reduction in the price of gas in January 1993 together with the 1 percentage point decrease in the general VAT rate in October 1992, through a carry-over effect, actually reduced inflation (in terms of the private consumption deflator) by ½ of a percentage point (Diagram 6). CPI inflation increased somewhat early this year, to 2.8 per cent (year-on-year) in May. However, underlying inflation decreased to 3.1 per cent (year-on-year) in April.

The labour market

The labour market, which has long been one of the weak points of the Dutch economy, has suffered appreciably from the economic downturn, although in a

22

delayed way. While in most other European countries employment in persons fell already in 1992, in the Netherlands it has continued to grow, albeit at a slower pace. To some extent, however, this relative resiliency of employment has been due to a further increase in part-time work, and in full-time equivalents employment did fall in 1993, for the first time since 1983. The lag with respect to the evolution of employment in Europe generally may have largely reflected the fact that the Dutch economy weakened later than the economies of surrounding countries. Unlike in previous cycles, this time there has been no significant reduction in hours worked per year. At the same time, the labour force has continued to grow at a fairly rapid pace – over $1\frac{1}{2}$ per cent per year – mainly because of demographic factors and the trend increase in the participation rate of women which, despite the downturn, has merely slowed. Moreover, as discussed in Part III, immigrants and especially asylum seekers have also contributed to increase the labour force.

The standardised unemployment rate continued to trend down until mid-1992, approaching $6\frac{1}{2}$ per cent, but then it rose steeply, to around 10 per cent early this year. By contrast, the unemployment rate in Europe, on average, began to rise already in early 1991 and its increase has been much less rapid (Diagram 3). Nonetheless, over the 1991-93 period, the gap between the Dutch unemployment rate and the higher European average rate widened considerably. This reflected the better growth performance of the Netherlands and its capacity to create jobs – even if only on a part-time basis – which has more than compensated for the fact that the Dutch labour force has continued to grow while that of other European countries has remained broadly stable or declined. As for the relatively sharp cyclical profile of the Dutch unemployment rate it may have been due to several factors. The long period of wage moderation and shortages of skilled labour apparently resulted in widespread "labour hoarding" when the economy began to slow in the early 1990s. After mid-1992, with rapidly rising wages and mounting evidence of a downturn, this gave way to a pronounced "labour shake-out". The need of a few large firms – including some major multinationals – to restructure, transfer production abroad and drastically cut jobs contributed to this labour shake-out.

Last year, unemployment rose over the whole range. A salient feature was an increase in the share of youth unemployment, after several years of gradual decline. Vacancies continued their rapid fall – from 110 000 or 1.6 per cent of

23

the labour force in early 1991 to about 32 000 or 0.5 per cent of the labour force in the fourth quarter of 1993. The share of vacancies with a low vocational level has also fallen. Finally, as discussed at some length in Part III, traditional measures of unemployment fail to portray fully Dutch labour-market problems. A broader concept ("broad unemployment") – including unemployed and inactive persons of working age receiving a social security benefit and persons enrolled in special job creation programmes – shows an unemployment rate of the order of 25 per cent of the broad labour force (in full-time equivalents). After several years of near-stability, this rate of unemployment began rising again already in 1992, and last year exceeded 26 per cent.

International competitiveness, foreign trade and the balance of payments

Despite progress towards wage moderation, the strength of the guilder put pressure on the international competitive position of the Dutch economy last year. Unit labour costs in manufacturing increased slightly less than in partner countries, but this advantage was more than offset by the appreciation of the currency, and relative unit labour costs in a common currency increased, bringing to nearly 6 per cent the cumulative deterioration of this indicator of competitiveness in 1992-93 (Diagram 7, panel A). Nonetheless, as noted, to remain competitive, Dutch exporters cut prices and reduced profit margins: export prices in a common currency apparently fell relative to partner countries, after having remained stable in 1992. However, import prices declined appreciably relative to domestic prices, in line with a well-established trend (Diagram 7, panel B). Given the stabilisation of the guilder and further progress towards wage moderation, the competitive position of Dutch firms, in terms of unit labour costs in a common currency, may have recovered somewhat in the first half of 1994; and profit margins may have been partially restored.

Trade flows in 1993 seem to have been primarily affected by the downturn in the domestic economy and in international trade. Although the introduction of the EC single market has created some statistical problems in this area, available data suggest that, reflecting the decline in domestic demand, the volume of merchandise imports fell. On the other hand, despite slack in relevant foreign markets, merchandise exports continued to grow, albeit at a very slow pace. As a

Diagram 7. **COMPETITIVENESS, TRADE AND THE CURRENT ACCOUNT**[1]

Index 1980 = 100

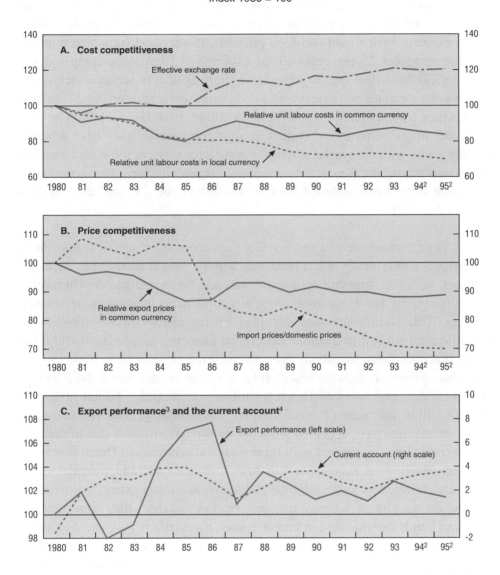

1. Due to the changeover in reporting systems for EC trade statistics, figures for 1993 must be regarded as being somewhat tentative.
2. Projections.
3. Ratio of volume of Dutch manufacturing exports to export market.
4. As a per cent of GDP.
Source: OECD Secretariat.

result, Dutch exporters may have gained market shares both in manufacturing and total goods, more than erasing losses recorded in 1992. In addition to the competitive pricing policy noted above, this outcome reflected the product mix of Dutch exports. Agricultural and food products, the demand for which remained buoyant, represent 25 per cent of total exports – a large share compared with other OECD countries. On the other hand, more cyclically-sensitive items, such as consumer durables and investment goods, represent a smaller share. The trade surplus may have increased to over Gld 15 billion, from Gld 12 billion in 1992. The other major items in the current account, on balance, may have remained broadly stable with the typical surplus in non-factor services more than matching net transfer payments. Hence, the current-account surplus (on a transaction basis) is estimated to have widened to Gld 16 billion, or $2^3/_4$ per cent of GDP (Tables 2 and 3).

A large current-account surplus is a permanent or structural feature in the Netherlands and typically it has been matched by ''autonomous'' private capital outflows, with little pressure on interest rates and the exchange rate. On balance, official financing has been small, with a modest trend increase in net external reserves. This equilibrium was disrupted by the 1992-93 EMS crisis, which caused capital outflow to dwindle and official financing to increase sharply. Last year's outcomes were essentially the result of exceptionally large flows during a very short period towards the end of July. A salient feature was a sharp increase in non-resident purchases of Dutch securities – from Gld 7 billion in 1992 to Gld 17 billion last year (Table 3). Apart from exchange rate considerations, Dutch shares may have appeared attractive to foreign investors due to their low price-earning ratios compared with other financial centres; and Dutch bonds may have benefitted from expectations of lower interest rates and potential capital gains. Dutch investors also contributed, although to a lesser extent, to the reduced outflow on account of security transactions. For instance, they were large net sellers of bonds denominated in French francs, especially in July and August. On the other hand, they were net buyers of DM-denominated bonds, presumably because of expectations that the unusually large negative interest differential between guilder-denominated bonds and DM-denominated bonds would narrow and result in larger capital gains on the latter than on the former. Altogether at Gld $12^1/_2$ billion, the reduction in capital outflows on account of security transactions was even larger than the positive swing on short-term (non-monetary)

Table 3. **Balance of payments**

Billion guilders

	1990	1991	1992	1993	Change 1993/92
A. Current account					
(on a transaction basis)[1]	18.4	14.2	11.9	16.0	4.1
Statistical discrepancies,					
including short-term trade credit	−5.6	−6.3	−1.8	0.3	2.1
B. Current account (on a cash basis)	**12.8**	**7.9**	**10.1**	**16.3**	**6.2**
C. Capital account	**−12.8**	**−8.0**	**0.7**	**−4.0**	**−4.7**
Non-monetary capital	−9.3	−16.5	−35.4	−4.9	30.5
of which:					
Securities transactions	−9.1	−2.0	−15.6	4.3	19.9
Foreign	−6.3	−9.4	−22.6	−18.7	3.9
Dutch	−2.8	7.4	7.0	23.0	16.0
Direct investment	−8.5	−13.0	−11.9	−6.5	5.5
Outward	−24.4	−22.0	−22.3	−19.1	3.2
Inward	15.9	9.0	10.3	12.6	2.3
Short-term capital[2]	2.8	−5.3	−5.7	−1.0	4.7
Monetary capital (bank transactions)	−3.5	8.5	36.2	0.9	−35.3
Short	−2.2	9.1	39.0	−0.1	−39.1
Long	−1.3	−0.6	−2.8	1.0	3.8
D. Official financing (B + C)[3]	**0.0**	**−0.1**	**10.8**	**12.4**	**1.5**
Foreign exchange	1.2	−0.2	9.1	13.2	4.1
Gold	−0.2	0.0	0.0	−6.2	−6.2
Ecus	−1.3	−0.2	0.4	6.0	5.5
Others	0.3	0.2	1.3	−0.6	−1.9

1. For 1993, Secretariat estimate.
2. Including errors and omissions.
3. + = increase in assets/decrease in liabilities.
Source: De Nederlandsche Bank; Quarterly bulletin 1993, No. 4.

capital transactions – from a sizeable outflow in 1992 to an inflow in 1993. The net outflow related to direct foreign investment also decreased markedly, although this may have primarily reflected factors other than exchange rate turbulence. At Gld 6¹/₂ billion, this outflow was at its lowest level since 1988. Inward direct investment increased somewhat, but remained well below the peak of a few years ago when it was boosted by business decisions in anticipation of the European single market. At the same time, Dutch firms reduced appreciably their direct investment abroad, presumably because of unsatisfactory economic conditions and prospects in many foreign countries. The fading of the single market effect may have affected outward investment too, especially since these flows are generally dominated by a few large multinational companies which, though Dutch-based, mainly operate abroad. Monetary flows (related to bank transactions) moved in an offsetting way compared to the rest of the capital account – with the very large inflows of 1992 virtually coming to a halt.

According to the rules of the ERM, the central bank intervened extensively in the foreign exchange market in 1993 to prevent the guilder from exceeding its upper fluctuation limits against the weak currencies. This type of intervention was especially important during the summer and particularly in the period imme-diately preceding the decision, at the beginning of August, to widen the ERM fluctuation margins. In addition, the central bank also engaged in "intramarginal intervention" – *i.e.* intervention which takes place before the upper or lower limits are reached – on behalf of other ERM currencies. As a result, most of the financing of the current-account surplus last year was again provided by an increase in official reserves – Gld 12 1/2 billion, virtually all in the form of foreign exchange.[5] Since the loosening of the ERM, Dutch capital flows have shown a tendency to resume a more normal pattern, but the net reflow of funds has been rather limited. Hence, official reserves have declined relatively little since their sudden, sharp increase last summer.

Short-term prospects

The outlook has distinctly improved over the past few months, and the rate of capacity utilisation has increased significantly. However, the industrial invest-ment surveys for 1994 are still weak. More generally, the recovery is likely to be restrained by the same factors which made the downturn less pronounced than in most other European countries – *i.e.* the structure of production of the Dutch economy. Economic policy, which is discussed in Part II, may, on balance, have a moderately expansionary impact on activity. Monetary conditions are projected to ease further, as interest rates continue to decline this year and next in line with German rates – although at the longer-end of the market the decline may be very slow. With respect to fiscal policy, the Government has decided to cut employ-ers' social security contributions to reduce labour costs and stimulate employ-ment; and to lower income taxes in order to promote wage moderation. Moreover, the Government has introduced a medium-term investment programme – the so-called "investment impulse" (see Part II).

GDP growth is projected to pick up only moderately this year before accelerating in 1995, to 2¾ per cent. The driving force of the upturn is buoyant world trade and, at a later stage, a recovery in domestic investment. Business investment may decline again this year, but less markedly than in 1993, as firms have almost fully adjusted to the lower level of demand. The rate of capacity utilisation is higher than in previous cyclical downturns, and despite an erosion of profitability there are no major balance-sheet problems in the business sector. This, combined with an improved sales outlook, better profit margins as a result of restructuring and wage moderation, and declining interest rates should lead to a rebound of investment in 1995. Moreover, investment in the energy sector is expected to be buoyant, and investment in the infrastructure for railways and other public transport under the recently introduced government "investment impulse" will be statistically recorded as business investment (Gld 3 billion in 1994-98). Residential investment, may also strengthen but less markedly. Housing construction in the unsubsidised sector should benefit from the better economic climate, remaining regional shortages and, due to lagged effects, recent declines in mortgage rates and increases in real rents. On the other hand, as in 1993, the construction of social dwellings may be largely determined and restrained by administrative and institutional factors, such as the October 1993 agreement making housing corporations largely independent of the government. This agreement has still to be ratified by Parliament. Although it is difficult to assess its likely impact on housing construction, there is a distinct possibility that, from now on, housing corporations might follow a more prudent investment strategy. Public investment is expected to be fairly buoyant partly as a result of the "investment impulse" which will result in the construction of new roads and waterways worth some Gld 2 billion in 1994-98.

Private consumption will be underpinned by an improved economic environment. The non-contractual savings ratio may drop further this year and then stabilise at a low level – around 1¼ per cent. The growth in exports (in volume) is expected to accelerate markedly in response to the pick up in world trade, but Dutch exporters may lose some market shares as they may use better cost conditions to restore profit margins. Imports are expected to rebound strongly, reflecting the recovery of domestic demand and the high import content of exports. Hence, *ex post*, the positive contribution of the foreign balance to GDP growth may remain unchanged, but the current-account surplus may nonetheless widen further, to 3½ per cent of GDP in 1995. A gradual recovery may have only a limited impact on the labour market and may not prevent the unemployment rate (on a yearly basis) from rising further this year, before declining slightly in 1995. Slack labour-market conditions should help achieve wage moderation as agreed by the social partners. Private compensation per employee is projected to increase by 2 per cent in 1995 and the rise in the private consumption deflator to edge down to 2 per cent.

As it is typically the case for a small, very open economy like the Netherlands, the projections are highly dependent on the conjunctural situation in neighbouring countries and the growth of international trade. But this time, the risks seem to be about balanced. On the downside, there is the possibility that the recent steep increase in long-term interest rates and further weakness in international stock and bond prices might sap confidence and result in weaker than expected consumption and investment. On the other hand, if the recent turbulence in financial markets were to prove short-lived, the prospect of a more rapid decline in interest rates in Europe than allowed for here could result in a stronger rebound in private fixed investment than projected.

II. Economic policies in a difficult environment

During the recent difficult period, characterised by an economic downturn and turbulence in the European Exchange Rate Mechanism (ERM), the Netherlands has continued to reap the benefits of its stable and rigorous economic policy. The anti-inflationary monetary policy based on the close link between the guilder and the Deutschemark has been a distinct success. Confidence in the guilder has been, if anything, strengthened by the two ERM crises: it enables the Netherlands to have the lowest interest rates possible over the longer term, although in 1992-93 it put pressure on the international competitiveness of Dutch firms. The Netherlands has also been more successful than most other European countries in pursuing fiscal consolidation – *i.e.* the reduction in the public sector budget deficit – despite the unfavourable conjunctural situation and rapidly rising unemployment. However, the public debt/GDP ratio is still not on a downward trend, as required to meet the Maastricht criteria; and the "collective burden" – *i.e.* the share of taxes and social security contributions in Net National Income – is one of the highest in the OECD area and remains well above the ceiling set by the Coalition Agreement of 1989. With a view to reducing the "collective burden" and to boosting employment, the Government has recently decided to revise upward its budget deficit target for 1994, and has announced a substantial reduction in taxes and social security contributions. With slack labour market conditions, efforts by the authorities to promote wage moderation have recently also been broadly successful. On the structural side, although new measures have been taken, notably in the area of competition policy and disability, progress has been slow and, on balance, this has been the aspect of economic policy which has progressed the least.

Monetary policy

The fundamental benefits and occasional strains of Dutch hard-currency policy anchored on the Deutschemark were once again evidenced by the ERM crisis of the summer of 1993. Unlike most other ERM countries, the Netherlands went through that turbulent period without experiencing either capital flights or upward pressure on its interest rates; and interest differentials with Germany remained negative even at the height of the crisis. Hence, the Dutch authorities did not face the dilemma of either defending the exchange rate or giving support to a weak economy, and monetary policy was able to stay its medium-term course of gradual easing. The strength of the guilder *vis-à-vis* other ERM currencies resulted in heavy intervention in the foreign exchange market by the central bank and a large increase in official reserves. This had a repercussion on domestic liquidity, although the authorities feel that it did not pose a problem for the conduct of monetary policy.

Dutch and international financial markets were quite calm in the first half of 1993. The guilder was generally slightly above its DM central rate in the upper half of the ERM narrow band, requiring no official intervention (Diagram 8). The

Diagram 8. **THE GUILDER AND THE DEUTSCHEMARK IN THE ERM BAND**

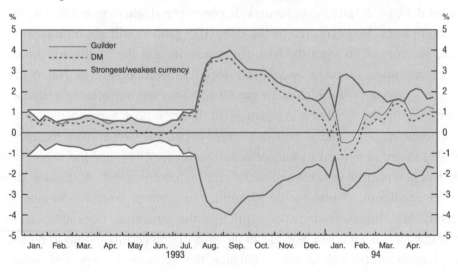

Source: OECD Secretariat.

central bank repeatedly reduced its official interest rates, broadly in line with the Bundesbank. Market rates declined appreciably, especially short-term ones, extending a trend which had started already in late 1992 (Diagram 9, panel A). The inverted yield curve flattened, and differentials with Germany became negative across the maturity spectrum, with short-term differentials widening to unusual levels (Diagram 9, panel B).

The situation changed drastically in July, when tensions within the ERM reappeared and rose rapidly. In the Netherlands, the typical capital outflows dried up and gave way to massive inflows, putting strong upward pressure on the guilder which moved to the ceiling of the narrow band. The central bank intervened in the foreign exchange market to prevent the guilder from exceeding the upper fluctuation limits *vis-à-vis* the weak currencies of the ERM. With unsettled market conditions, it would probably have required sizeable interest rate cuts to affect capital flows, and such a unilateral move could have had unforseen consequences on credibility in Dutch monetary policy. Hence, the authorities preferred to rely on intervention. This was massive, although short-lived: for the third quarter as a whole, official reserves increased by Gld 12.4 billion or nearly 3 per cent of the money supply. While remaining above its DM-central rate, the guilder lost some ground against this currency, and the negative short-term interest differential with Germany was largely erased. At the beginning of August, the ERM fluctuation margins were widened to 15 per cent of the central rates; but in a bilateral agreement between the Netherlands and Germany it was decided that the guilder-Deutschemark fluctuation margins would remain unchanged at $2^{1}/_{4}$ per cent.

This loosening of the ERM was followed, at first, by a sizeable appreciation of the guilder *vis-à-vis* most other ERM currencies, but then pressure progressively abated and the gap between the guilder – which generally remained the strongest ERM currency – and the weakest currency narrowed, from around 8 per cent in September to 4 per cent at the end of 1993. Hence, the guilder, in effective terms, ended the year virtually where it had started it, and its year-on-year appreciation was limited to $2^{3}/_{4}$ per cent – only slightly more than in 1992. Throughout this turbulent period, Dutch monetary authorities continued their policy of prudent easing. As a result, the decline in domestic interest rates was significant in 1993: the rate on the central bank's advances (the most important official rate) fell from 8.25 per cent to 5.5 per cent, and money market rates from

Diagram 9. INTEREST RATES AND EXCHANGE RATES

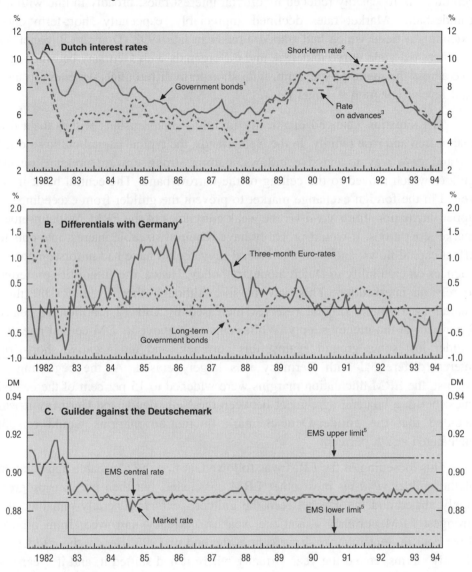

1. 5-8 years.
2. 3-month loans to local authorities.
3. Main official rate of Central Bank.
4. Dutch rates minus German rates.
5. Since August 1993 this is a bilateral German-Dutch arrangement.
Source: OECD, Financial Statistics Monthly and Main Economic Indicators.

8.6 to 5.7 per cent. The decline in long-term rate – from 7.3 to 5.7 per cent – was only a little less pronounced.

In tandem with the Deutschemark, the guilder weakened within the ERM early this year, pointing to some unwinding of speculative positions and net outflows of capital. But in March, the guilder moved back to the top of the band, and since then it has remained one of the strongest ERM currencies. While short-term rates have continued to decline, long-term rates have rebounded markedly – by some 150 basis points – and the yield curve has become upward sloping again. The weakness in Dutch bonds has been broadly in line with developments in global bond markets, with prices beginning to decline in early February when the Federal Reserve Bank started raising US short-term interest rates. While at the short end of the market the negative differential with Germany has nearly disappeared, at the longer end the differential has become positive (Diagram 10). This may reflect a decline in German inflation relative to Dutch inflation. Nonetheless, Dutch interest rates remain among the lowest in Europe, both in nominal and real terms. Nominal interest rates are lower only in Switzerland.

Progress towards European Monetary Union (EMU) has prompted the central bank to reconsider the composition of its reserves. In view of the importance of its official gold stock, compared with other industrialised countries and in relation to GDP, the central bank arranged, already in the autumn of 1992, to sell 400 tonnes of gold (for $4.3 billion), thereby reducing its gold stock by nearly one-fourth, from 1.707 to 1.307 tonnes. This operation was settled and reflected in the bank's balance sheet in February 1993. Combined with last July's intervention in exchange markets it has brought the share of gold in the central bank's total gold and foreign exchange holdings more into line with the EC average.

The authorities no longer have explicit monetary targets. At the end of the 1980s, they shifted from the "liquidity ratio" – i.e. the growth of the broadly defined domestic money supply relative to national income in nominal terms – to the exchange rate as the intermediate target of monetary policy. Domestic liquidity conditions remained broadly satisfactory in 1993, although the year-on-year rate of growth of the money supply (M3H) accelerated somewhat – to 7.1 from 6.3 per cent in 1992. Since at the same time economic activity weakened, the ratio between the rate of growth of money and nominal GDP approached 4, compared with less than 2 in 1992 (and 1989 when the money supply grew by nearly 11 per cent, the record of the recent period). About half of last year's

Diagram 10. INTEREST DIFFERENTIALS WITH GERMANY[1]

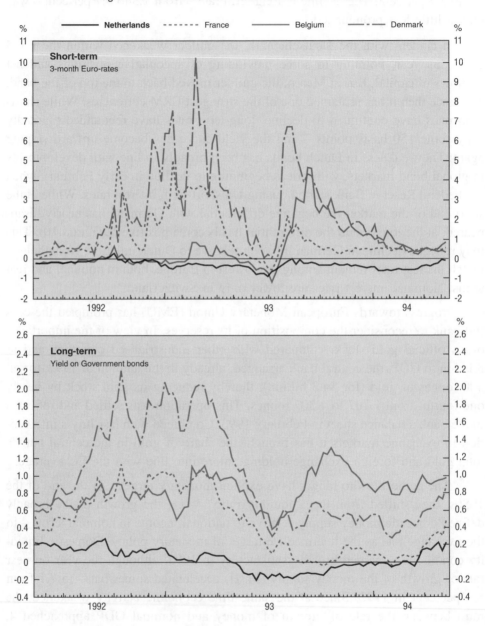

1. Break in series in July 1993.
Source: OECD Secretariat.

increase in the money supply was accounted for by external transactions – *i.e.* a surplus in the balance of non-monetary transactions (the current account plus non-monetary capital). Commercial banks' net money creating operations expanded at a rate of 8 per cent, about the same as in 1992. As a result of the economic slowdown short-term lending to the business sector declined, but long-term lending increased markedly, largely a reflection of the surge in mortgage loans on dwellings.

In order to mop up excess liquidity in the money market and to keep credit institutions dependent on its credit facilities (quota scheme, special loans), in special cases the central bank uses the (interest-bearing) money market cash reserve requirement. In July 1993, given the suddenness and size of official intervention in the exchange market, the money market cash reserve requirement had to be complemented by other instruments, notably currency swaps between the central bank and commercial banks. Moreover, since the cash reserve requirement is supposed to be used for only short periods, early this year the central bank began issuing special money market paper, (Nederlandsche Bank Certificates) to ensure a more permanent ''sterilisation'' of the excess liquidity created last summer.

In 1994-95, short-term interest rates are projected to continue to decline in line with German rates. Long rates may also decline again, following their upsurge in the first half of 1994, but this decline may be very slow. Interest differentials with Germany may narrow somewhat, with both the negative differential at the short end of the market and the positive differential at the long end moving towards zero. More settled conditions in foreign exchange markets, and notably in the ERM, should encourage a resumption of large net capital outflows. The growth of the money supply should thus abate and be more in line with the trend growth in money demand and nominal GDP.

Budget policy

The Coalition Accord of 1989 commits the Government to reducing the central government financial deficit according to a fixed time schedule: *i.e.* a reduction of $1/2$ percentage point of Net National Income (NNI) a year, to $3^1/4$ per cent in 1994. Furthermore, it stipulates that the collective burden should not exceed its 1990 level as expected at the time of the Coalition Accord.[6] Within these limits, the Government is striving to meet four additional objectives through fiscal policy: *i.e.* wage moderation – by lowering taxes; equitable income distribution; a redressment of the incentive balance between working and not working; and an improvement of the economic infrastructure. Over the past four years, the Government has been successful in bringing down the general government deficit (according to the EMU definition), from 5.0 per cent of GDP in 1990 to 2.9 per cent in 1993, in sharp contrast to other EC countries where budget deficits have risen rapidly in the worsening economic environment. However, the collective burden increased by more than 3 percentage points of NNI over the period 1990-93. Political priorities seem to have changed recently. In view of progress achieved in reducing the deficit and of rapidly rising unemployment, the Government has revised the deficit target upward to $3^{3}/_{4}$ per cent of NNI in 1994. Moreover, at the beginning of 1994, the Government announced substantial reductions in taxes and social security contributions for 1994 and 1995, amounting to GLD 5 billion or 1 per cent of GDP in 1995.

There are pros and cons to targeting actual rather than cyclically adjusted or structural deficits. On the one hand, actual targets have the advantage of defining a clear commitment by the authorities and may result in large confidence effects in the financial markets. On the other hand, pursuit of actual targets may force the Government to offset the automatic stabilisers with discretionary fiscal policy measures. This was clearly shown in the recent economic slowdown when the official Budgets were overtaken by downward revisions in economic activity.

Recent developments

The 1993 Budget was quickly overcome by economic events. It initially assumed economic growth of 2 per cent and aimed at reducing the central government deficit and collective burden in line with the targets set out in the 1989 Coalition Accord. At the same time, the Government tried to maintain purchasing power by increasing both social security benefits and the general deduction on income taxes.

Due to weaker than expected economic activity, estimated tax revenues were revised downwards, inducing the Government to introduce three additional fiscal packages. Total budgetary savings amounted to 0.8 per cent of GDP (Gld 4.7 billion), including a freeze on social benefits and cuts in central government expenditure which were proportionately divided over the ministries. However, a large part of these budget cuts (Gld 1.1 billion) stemmed from one-off measures such as delaying government payments and selling of government property (0.5 per cent of GDP). Moreover, the Government withdrew the general direct tax reduction announced in the 1993 Budget and completely refrained from correcting tax brackets for inflation.

As a result of the tight policy stance, government consumption growth remained subdued in 1993, at 1.8 per cent against 4.6 per cent in 1992. Government employment was virtually stable and compensation of civil servants increased by 1.8 per cent. In line with the 1991 Midterm Review measures, subsidies for social housing were reduced through higher rents (a 5½ per cent annual rate of increase). Helped by lower EC agriculture subsidies, total subsidies declined by 4 per cent. However, an unexpectedly large inflow of asylum seekers led to additional expenditure, and the interest on the public debt increased faster than expected.

The Government was less successful in controlling social security and health care outlays, which are administered by industrial boards, municipalities and other public boards. Although benefits were nominally frozen in 1993, social security outlays rose by 5 per cent. This reflected an upsurge in the number of unemployment beneficiaries and a renewed increase in the inflow of beneficiaries to the disability scheme.[7] Moreover, there were budget slippage in the health care sector, mainly in hospitals and pharmaceuticals, despite the recently introduced pharmaceuticals insurance reform.[8]

Despite the weak economy, the tax revenue outcome was much more favourable than foreseen in early 1993. Total tax revenues exceeded the 1993 Spring Note projection by Gld 5.2 billion (0.9 per cent of GDP). A large proportion of this direct tax windfall – Gld 3.4 billion – is considered by the authorities as being temporary, reflecting a shortening of the tax payment's term due to the reorganisation and computerisation of the tax department. However, the improved efficiency of the tax department has also led to a somewhat broader corporate tax base. The additional revenues stemming from indirect taxes are believed to be permanent, reflecting a level of private consumption expenditure higher than expected. In order to fine-tune the central budget deficit between 1993 and 1994, the central Government increased the public expenditure on a cash basis for 1993 – and decreased it for 1994 – by advancing payment of Gld 5.3 billion to various insurance funds.[9] As a result, the central Government achieved its 1993 deficit target, and the general government net borrowing declined from 3.5 per cent of GDP in 1992 to 2.9 per cent in 1993 (Table 4). But the collective burden increased by 1 percentage point of NNI, and the debt/GDP ratio rose slightly to 81½ per cent.

Budget outlook for 1994 and 1995

The Government has decided to slow down fiscal consolidation in 1994,[10] and to aim at a stable central government deficit – implying an upward revision of the 1994 official target to 3¾ per cent of NNI. Moreover, the financing of expenditure relies more on one-off revenues – *i.e.* the sale of government property such as KPN (Dutch National Telecommunication Enterprise)[11] and shares of ING-bank (Internationale Nederlanden Group). Coupled with the above men-

Table 4. **Appropriation account for general government**

	1989	Average 1990-92	1993	1994[1]	1995[1]
	In per cent of GDP	Annual percentage change			
Current receipts	45.2	6.9	4.4	1.0	2.5
Total direct taxes	13.9	10.3	8.3	−16.1[2]	2.5
On households	10.7	12.1	7.8	−17.0[2]	1.2
On business	3.2	3.6	10.3	−12.5	7.1
Social security contributions	18.8	4.8	3.5	14.0[2]	0.5
Indirect taxes	12.5	6.8	0.9	4.2	5.6
Disbursements	47.9	7.3	3.0	2.8	2.4
Government consumption	14.8	4.3	1.9	2.1	2.4
Wages and salaries	10.2	3.9	2.4	2.0	2.4
Expenditure excluding wages	4.6	5.3	0.9	2.3	2.2
Subsidies	3.5	1.9	−4.2	−4.5	−28.3
Net property income	2.1	6.2	7.1	13.4	30.4
Current transfers	26.6	8.3	4.3	2.5	2.5
Capital transactions	−1.6	−27.6	7.0	13.1	−5.7
of which:					
Gross investment	2.6	6.3	0.0	11.2	5.8
Net lending (per cent of GDP)	−4.7	−3.7	−2.9	−3.9	−3.7

1. Projections.
2. A neutral tax shift of Gld 2 billion decreased household taxes and increased social security contributions.
Source: OECD Secretariat.

40

tioned expenditure shift between 1993 and 1994, these non-recurrent factors represent 1½ per cent of GDP.[12] All considered, according to the OECD Secretariat, the net general government deficit on a national account basis may rise to 3.9 per cent of GDP in 1994; on the basis of announced policies it could then decline to 3.7 per cent in 1995, as economic growth accelerates. While this is not far from the Maastricht target, the debt/GDP ratio would rise further.

The easing of the fiscal stance in 1994 is mainly reflected in a lowering of tax and social security contributions and a boost in public investment (Table 5). In order to keep the actual central government budget deficit stable, the tax reductions – for 1994 largely a decrease in employers' contributions[13] – are of the same magnitude as the permanent part of the 1993 tax windfall and the expected cyclical improvement in tax revenues (Gld 1.5 billion for 1994). Hence, the Government is once again offsetting the automatic stabilisers in an effort to support the recovery and promote wage moderation. Furthermore, in 1994 the Government aims at maintaining equal income distribution by not correcting the tax brackets for inflation and at redressing the incentive balance between working and not working by increasing the standard worker's deduction.

Current public expenditure growth remains restricted at 1.5 per cent in 1994, much below nominal GDP growth. The 1994 Budget includes expenditure cuts of Gld 7.4 billion (1.2 per cent of GDP) and new expenditure measures of Gld 1.6 billion. The most important expenditure reductions are the freeze on social security benefits and government wages (Gld 2.5 billion) and budget cuts proportionately divided over the department budgets (Gld 2.7 billion). The reform of the sickness scheme, implemented in January 1994, is expected to cut social security outlays by a further Gld 1 billion.[14] New expenditure measures include public investment, public safety and active labour market policies. Moreover, the Government has introduced a medium-term investment programme (the so-called "investment impulse"), amounting to Gld 5 billion (nearly 1 per cent of GDP), for the period 1994-98, to be financed through the Fund for Improvement of the Economic Structure (FES). The Fund will support major infrastructure projects and business investment of significant national importance, such as the Betuwe freight railway between Rotterdam and Germany and the high-speed railway link between Belgium and Amsterdam.[15] The revenues of the Fund consist of the so-called "common area" gas revenues,[16] possible excess revenues from privatisation and extra revenues of the export of natural gas.

Table 5. **Overview of most important fiscal measures in 1994 and 1995**

Billion guilders

	1994	1995
A. Budget expenditure cuts	**7.4**	**5.0**
of which:		
Cuts in department's budgets	2.7	1.7
Nominal freeze of benefits and government wages	2.5	1.2
Housing subsidies	0.5	0.3
Social benefits	0.6	0.7
"Efficiency operation"	0.2	
Other	0.8	1.2
B. Budget expenditure increases	**–1.6**	**–0.7**
of which:		
Public investment	0.6	0.5
Active labour market policies	0.3	0.2
Other	0.7	0.1
C. Budget tax increases	**2.1**	**0.5**
of which:		
No correction to tax brackets for inflation	1.2	
Environmental levies		0.5
Increases in excise taxes	0.9	
D. Budget tax decreases	**–2.2**	**–0.4**
of which:		
Increase in worker's deduction on taxable income	–0.5	–0.1
Decrease in the first bracket tax rate	–0.9	–0.2
R&D facility	–0.2	–0.1
Other	–0.6	
E. Once-off measures and privatisations	**8.7**	**6.3**
F. February 1994 tax decreases	**–2.1**	**–2.9**
of which:		
Decrease in employers' unemployment insurance contributions	–1.4	–0.6
Decrease in the first bracket tax rate	–0.3	–2.3
Lowering of taxes on business and capital income	–0.4	

Source: Ministry of Finance.

Major risks for both the 1994 Budget and the 1995 Budget are the continuing rapid increase in unemployment beneficiaries, and the large inflow of asylum seekers and other budget overruns. Although the 1995 Budget will be presented by a new Government taking office after the elections, the current Government has already announced a fiscal package of 0.3 per cent of GDP, which only partly covers this expected extra expenditure. Once again, savings consist of a less than full correction of departmental budgets for inflation and restricting the wage bill for civil servants.

Fiscal consolidation in a longer term perspective

In response to the dramatic increase in the budget deficit in the early 1980s, the Government embarked on a new course in 1983. The main aim was a major reduction in the actual central government financial deficit (on a cash basis) according to a fixed time schedule. Initially, this policy was successful in bringing down the budget deficit: it fell from more than 8.9 per cent of GDP in 1983 to 5.7 per cent in 1986 (Diagram 11). In the period 1986-90, however, at a time when the cyclical economic situation improved considerably, budget overruns and additional expenditure were easily financed by cyclically high tax revenue without violating the actual deficit targets. As a result, according to OECD Secretariat calculations, the positive change in the cyclical component of the budget balance was, for a large part, offset by a negative change in the structural component (see Diagram 12).[17] The structural deficit rose, and despite strong economic growth, the public debt continued to rise. In the subsequent downturn, the opposite happened. The high structural deficit limited the scope for allowing the automatic stabilisers to work and required the Government to take discretionary measures to respect the actual targets. During the latest government period 1989-94, budget projections were overtaken four times by downward revisions in economic activity, forcing the Government to introduce fiscal packages, additional to the initial budget. In terms of budget savings measures, these additional packages were of greater importance than the original budgets. They amounted to 5 per cent of GDP in the last Government period, and as a result the structural deficits improved by 3 percentage points of GDP.

In addition to having a pro-cyclical impact on domestic demand, the strategy of actual targets with a rigid time schedule has disturbed the smooth working of the budgetary process and may have had an upward bias on tax revenues and distorted the composition of general government expenditure. During cyclical downturns, direct measures had to be taken in order to get the deficit back on schedule. This budget process may have skewed budget savings towards tax increases and cuts in government expenditure items over which the Government has the best control, *i.e.* public investment, subsidies and consumption. Despite

Diagram 11. **FISCAL CONSOLIDATION
IN A HISTORICAL PERSPECTIVE**

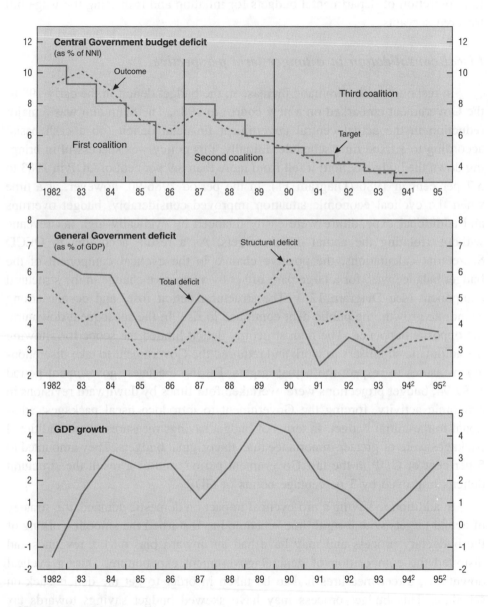

1. Official Dutch projections.
2. OECD Secretariat projections.
Sources: Ministry of Finance, Central Planning Bureau and OECD Secretariat.

Diagram 12. **CHANGES IN CYCLICAL AND STRUCTURAL BUDGET BALANCES**[1]

Percentage change in the structural
component of the budget balance

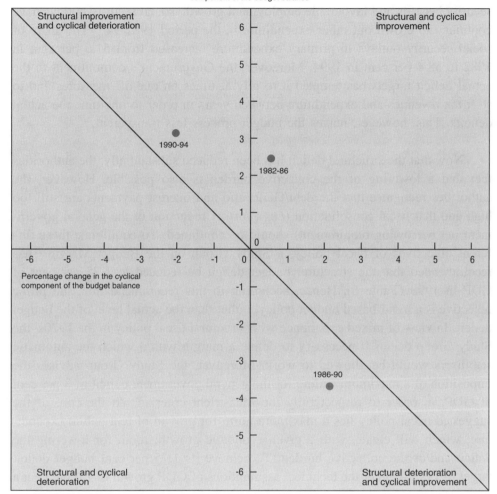

1. General government budget balances as a per cent of GDP. The budget balance can be decomposed into a cyclical and non-cyclical, or structural, component. The structural component is derived by calculating the value of all budget items if GDP were at its trend level. The cyclical component is derived by the difference.
Source: OECD Secretariat.

efforts to reform the disability scheme, general government transfers to households continued to increase as a percentage of total government expenditure. True, the increase over the last four years may have been largely due to rising unemployment. However, despite an almost constant nominal freeze on social security benefits and favourable employment growth, social security outlays have continued to crowd out other expenditure in the period 1982-94.[18] The share of social security outlays in primary expenditure increased from 51.6 per cent in 1982 to 58.4 per cent in 1994. Moreover, the Government's commitment to the actual deficit targets has tempted it to rely at times on one-off measures and to shift tax revenues and expenditure between years in order to fine-tune the actual deficits. This, however, makes the budget process less transparent.

Now that the structural deficit has been reduced substantially, the authorities feel that a lowering of the collective burden is also possible. However, the authorities recognise that the debt/GDP ratio and interest payments are still too high and that fiscal consolidation (*i.e.* a further reduction of the general government net borrowing requirement) should be continued. To equilibrate these different objectives of fiscal policy, a Study Group on the Budget Margin[19] has recommended that the structural budget deficit be reduced to 1.75 per cent of GDP in 1998 (Table 6). Hence, according to this recommendation, the prime objective is a trend-based budget policy, rather than the actual level of the budget deficit. In view of mixed experience with structural fiscal policy in the 1970s, the Study Group deems it necessary to define a margin within which the automatic stabilisers would be allowed to work. Moreover, the Study Group advises the imposition of a maximum ceiling for the general government deficit of 3 per cent of GDP, in order to respect fully the Maastricht criteria.[20] At the core of the suggested fiscal policy lies a maximum norm for growth of real public expenditure, which will create, with a given economic growth, room for lowering the deficit and/or the collective burden. To achieve its 1.75 per cent budget deficit target in 1998 – under the technical assumptions of GDP growth of 1¾ per cent a year as indicated in the Central Planning Bureau "cautious" medium-term scenario and a reduction of the collective burden of 2 percentage points of GDP – the Study Group has calculated that real expenditure growth should be restricted to 0.5 per cent a year. Even so, if the budget deficit were to stabilise at 1¾ per cent after 1998, the EMU requirement of a debt/GDP ratio of 60 per cent would not be achieved before 2010.

Table 6. **Fiscal consolidation beyond 1994: key figures from the Study Group on the Budget Margin**

	1994	1995	1998	1995-98	Memorandum 1991-1994
Assumptions					
GDP growth in current prices				4.6	3.5
Real GDP growth				1.75	1.3
GDP deflator				2.75	2.2
Tax progression factor				1.0	1.0
Interest rates (long-term)				7.0	7.4
Results					
Net lending general government (as a percentage of GDP)	−3.1	−2.9	−1.8		
Debt/GDP ratio	79.6	79.7	74.6		
Collective burden (as a percentage of GDP)	46.5	46.1	44.5		
of which: Social Security contributions	20.1	19.6	19.1		
Interest payments (as a percentage of GDP)	6.2	6.0	5.8		
Nominal growth of general government expenditure				3.25	4.2
of which: Social Security outlays				0.3	5.1
Real growth of general government expenditure				0.5	2.0

Source: Ninth report of the Study Group on the Budget Margin, "Towards a trend-based budget policy".

Competition policy

The Government has started a major overhaul of competition policy and legislation. As noted in the previous Survey, until recently the Netherlands did not have a very strict competition policy and its legislation in this area was quite different from that of most other OECD countries: for instance, cartels and other collusive agreements were not banned in principle. Moreover, licensing rules were widespread, restrictive and complex; and in the public sector, administered prices played a major role. As a result, the degree of competition seemed rather low, especially in sectors not exposed to international trade. The growth performance in the 1980s was somewhat below the EC average and particularly mediocre in terms of per capita GDP. However, the price level of gross domestic product in 1990, was virtually in line with the EC and OECD averages, after being significantly above it in 1980;[21] and, at the macroeconomic level, profits were not abnormally high by international standards. But it is difficult to determine to what extent these macroeconomic results were due to the state of competition, and to what extent they were due to other factors, such as problems in the labour market and the very low participation rate (see Part III), wage moderation, and monetary policy and exchange rate policy. On the other hand, the Survey found strong microeconomic evidence of distortions and welfare losses due to weak competition. This has been especially the case in the sheltered sector of the economy – notably the construction sector – where profits have been consistently higher and more stable than in the exposed sector; prices have been significantly above the EC average; and wages have substantially exceeded those in the rest of the economy.

In the late 1980s, the Government started preparing a complete overhaul of competition policy, and stepped up implementation within the existing system based on the Economic Competition Act of 1956. The aim is to align Dutch competition policy with the EC and make it better suited to a very open, dynamic economy. This is to be done gradually, with the transition period extending over several years. As regards competition narrowly defined, the Government has been following two parallel tracks. The first one concerns the introduction of three general prohibition decrees based on the existing Economic Competition Act, each one of them dealing with a specific group of restrictive agreements and all of them containing the possibility of an exception in individual cases – with criteria based on article 85.3 of the EC Treaty. The first decree prohibits, as from 1 July 1993, horizontal price agreements. It was expected that most of the 150-odd such agreements which were on the Cartel Register at end-1992 would ask for an exception. However, it turned out that many registered price agreements were no longer operative (*i.e.* did not exist any more) and only 50 requests for exception were submitted. In some 30 cases the Government – after seeking the advice of the Economic Competition Commission – has already decided to refuse an exception. No exception has been granted up to now. The remaining cases should be decided before the end of 1994, well ahead of what was expected when the previous Survey was finalised. Two other decrees will prohibit, as from 1 June 1994, market sharing agreements (broadly defined), and collusive tendering (for all sectors, including the building and construction sector).

In addition, the Government submitted amendments of the Economic Competition Act to Parliament in September 1993. The most important amendments concern improved possibilities of legal action against restrictive practices which are not based on legally binding agreements (informal collusion). As a result, the scope of the law has been widened to cover all liberal professions which, through professional organisations, have a strong legal self-regulatory power over their members, allowing them to restrain competition, set uniform tariffs, and preserve high profits. For instance, the authorities estimate that for this reason the cost of public notary services is Gld 300-400 million "too high". The Government is expected to give the public notaries a transition period of a couple of years over which to phase out their cartelized pricing practices. Finally, as noted in the previous Survey, the authorities are also in the process of introducing a new, sharply revised and liberalised Establishment Law. Although a few changes have already been introduced, full implementation is still expected, at the earliest in 1996.

The second track is concerned with the introduction of a completely new competition law which will be based on the principles of the European rules of competition: restrictive agreements and practices will be prohibited as well as abuses of dominant positions by one or more parties. This approach is more general than the existing Competition Law complemented by the three decrees mentioned above, and in practice the difference will be significant. In order to take action, the authorities will no longer have to decide which form of restrictive agreements they are faced with – *i.e.* horizontal price agreements, market sharing agreements, or collusive tendering – which is often difficult to establish; and a dominant firm will not simply have to stop an abusive practice found unlawful, as it is actually the case, but it will be punishable from the moment the practice started. Also, enforcement by criminal law will be replaced by administrative enforcement, providing more flexibility. Before submitting the new legislation to Parliament, the Government will have to wait for the advice of the Social Economic Council (which is expected within a few months), and the Commission on Economic Competition. All considered, the new Act may not take effect before 1997. This is why, to save time, the Government has opted for the two-track approach. Finally, as noted in the previous Survey, the authorities are also considering whether in a small, very open economy like the Netherlands, it would be appropriate to control mergers and acquisitions and to establish an independent competition agency. It is too early to assess the impact of these various measures on the degree of competition and on the economy. While in some respect progress on the legal-institutional side may have been faster than expected, aligning Dutch competition policy with the EC will remain a gradual and long process.

As for competition in a broader sense, the authorities are aware of the need to rely more on the market mechanism in public sector activities. Existing legislation and regulatory schemes are being reviewed, especially for heavily regulated sectors such as housing, public health, public transport, and public utilities. But major decisions are not expected before the new Government comes into office.

Other structural policies

The Dutch health care system is in the midst of a major reform, the outline of which was provided by the Dekker Committee in 1987. It identified the following fundamental shortcomings of the Dutch health care system: a limited possibility of substitution between different types of care; complexities and inefficiencies caused by the mixed private-public system; and a lack of incentives for efficiency, cost awareness and competition; and insufficiently defined responsibilities in the mixed private-public system. The Committee based its advice on three central premises: integration of provisions in the field of health care and social care; more efficient and flexible health care; and a shift from government regulations to regulation through market forces. It proposed a single compulsory basic insurance scheme, covering about 85 per cent of total health care, to be financed mostly by an income-related premium but also by a flat-rate premium. The latter would presumably differ from insurance company to insurance company, depending on their efficiency. In 1988, the Government decided to implement a modified version of the Dekker proposal, consisting of a compulsory basic insurance scheme, covering 85 per cent of total health provisions, but with a somewhat different system of financing (75 per cent of total health cost to be financed by an income-related premium and 25 per cent by a flat-rate premium). A plan of action was set out with a view to completing the transition by 1992.

The first phase of the reform started in 1989. The exceptional medical expenses scheme (AWBZ) was used as a vehicle for setting up the basic insurance scheme. In May 1990, the new centre-left Government announced that it would continue, albeit more slowly than had been envisaged previously, with the main thrust of the reform (Simons Plan). Some important changes based on policy considerations were proposed, however, notably the extension of the basic insurance to all essential care in order to encourage substitution between different types of services. As a consequence, the content of the basic insurance package was enlarged to cover about 90-95 per cent of total health care expenditure (instead of 85 per cent). The ratio between the compulsory, income-related part of the premium for basic insurance and the negotiable flat-rate part was increased to 85/15.

The second phase of the reform started at the beginning of 1992. Among other measures, it introduced the so-called "functional descriptions" of some care provisions, and conditions creating more competition among the providers of health care. In June 1992, however, the Government issued a document *(Well-considered Modernisation of the Health Care System)* expressing the view that the Simons Plan might be too ambitious, and suggested a more moderate step-by-step approach. As a result, the transfer of several care provisions to the basic insurance scheme was postponed, and measures were announced to increase financial incentives of the consumer and to stabilise the solidarity-payment required from all private insured persons to share in the cost of insuring persons with a high health risk (mainly elderly people). But opposition against the reform continued to grow. In November 1992, the Government and the coordinating organisations of private and social health insurers signed a memorandum of understanding on cost developments and bottlenecks in the deregulation ("modernisation") of the health care system. It was agreed that an independent committee would investigate the proposed budgeting of insurance companies. In June 1993, the Government decided to postpone the third phase of the reform from the beginning of 1994 to the beginning of 1996, thereby leaving all further essential decisions in this area to the Government which will come into office after the elections of May 1994. One reason for the postponement was the conclusion of the independent committee that the Simons Plan's system of budgeting insurance companies for every insured person on the basis of a set of objective criteria was too complicated and should have been substituted with a system with a larger flat-rate premium and a smaller income-related premium.

In sum, serious doubts have emerged concerning key elements of the envisaged health care system. These have centred on the complicated system of budgeting of insurers as well as on the limited degree of competition which has been achieved both on the supply side of the health care market and between insurers (in the execution of the basic insurance scheme). The latter element has mainly reflected the relative unimportance of the flat-rate premium compared with the income-related premium.

Since 1983, the Government has been engaged in several "efficiency operations", the third one of which covers the years 1991-94, and involves both the central government and local authorities. It aims at both enhancing productivity within each ministry and department, and restructuring activities in the public sector as a whole, so as to abolish duplication of work and to decentralise tasks.[22] The target is the elimination, mainly through attrition, of some 6 000 jobs in full-time equivalents (about 4 per cent of central government employment), and the reduction of total public expenditures by some $1/2$ per cent in 1994. Last year, the cumulative reduction in jobs due to the third "efficiency operation" reached 2 700, and the authorities expect this figure to approach 5 500 this year.

In the environment area, the main focus of policy has been the implementation of the National Environment Policy Plan (NEPP) of 1991. Recent developments have included: compulsory partition of green household waste; seven agreements on energy saving with industrial and agricultural sectors; programmes on chrome and radon; and covenants with industry and commerce on the collection of batteries. In December 1993, the Government presented 3 new policy plans: NEPP 2, Product and Environment, and the Memorandum on Energy Conservation II. Each plan contains the specific measures which have to be taken. NEPP 2 and the Memorandum on Energy Conservation II confirm the goals of NEPP I and focus on execution and maintenance to reach them. Product and Environment contains a new environmental policy in the area of product information, based on the notion that, in order to choose, consumers need to know environmental aspects of products.

Dutch industrial policy aims at creating general conditions that favour the competitiveness of industry. Technological innovation is at the heart of this policy. The amounts involved are limited and represent only $1/4$ of a per cent of GDP – well below the EC average. In January 1993, the Government introduced an Industry Facility to increase the supply of high-risk or venture capital for high-tech projects of medium-size and large firms. According to the authorities, although on the whole there is no shortage of capital in the Netherlands, in specific segments of the capital market problems exist with respect to the availability of venture capital. This may partly be due to the lack of investment banks and the dominant position of institutional funds. The Facility is a public-private partnership: it will be financed by private investors (78 per cent) and the government (22 per cent). The private sector is represented by four banks, eight insurance companies and fourteen pension funds. The Facility will provide several forms of risk capital at market conditions. In each case, the amount will vary from a minimum of Gld 10 million to a maximum of Gld 50 million. To be eligible a firm should be "important" for the Dutch economic structure; be well managed and offer a good prospect for long-term profitability; have an obvious need for risk capital; and have no other possibilities for financing this capital need. The Industry Facility aims at complementing existing facilities for small firms which provide guarantees for loans and venture capital.

III. The labour market: a very high non-employment rate

When the Dutch labour market was last discussed in detail in the 1998/89 Survey, the employment/unemployment situation – despite positive trends – was unsatisfactory, and it was noted that labour-market problems were likely to remain important in the 1990s as a result of several factors: a sustained growth of labour supply requiring a continued strong growth of labour demand to make inroads into unemployment; structural changes placing new demands on the labour market to absorb a growing number of women seeking part-time jobs, to adjust to the rising share of older workers, and to meet the need for a more skilled and qualified labour force. This prognosis, by and large, has been born out by events. Moreover, over the past couple of years, additional developments – such as the cyclical downturn and the prospect of only moderate growth in coming years, heightened competition from non-OECD countries, and a rising flow of immigrants – have further aggravated the situation, especially at the lower end of the labour market. At the same time, the budgetary cost of unemployment in all its forms has become increasingly hard to sustain given the need for fiscal consolidation, for reduction in the collective burden, and for a better ''quality'' of public expenditure. For all these reasons, as well as for pressing human and social considerations, the employment/unemployment question is now at the top of the policy agenda in the Netherlands, as in most other OECD countries.

Main features of the labour market: historical evolution and current situation

Overview

Labour market performance has deteriorated markedly over the past two decades, despite a period of rapid job creation in the second half of the 1980s.

Recorded unemployment[23] rose from less than 1 per cent of the labour force in 1970 to around 10 per cent in early 1994, with swings which have been among the largest in the OECD. While the increase in unemployment by over 3 percentage points since mid-1992 may be largely cyclical, many indicators suggest that structural unemployment has risen strongly since previous cycles. Moreover, the effective rate of unemployment is considerably higher than the recorded one: for instance, including all unemployed and inactive persons of working age receiving a social security benefit and persons enrolled in special job creation programmes ("broad unemployment"),[24] the rate currently exceeds 26 per cent, compared with less than 8 per cent in 1970. The large withdrawals of workers associated with broad unemployment have curbed the increase in the labour force, but the growth in employment has been even lower, especially in the first half of the 1980s, and the gap has never been fully erased. A key feature of the Dutch labour market has been the increasing importance of part-time work. Hence, even though the participation rate as conventionally measured has continued to increase and is close to the European average, the participation rate in full-time equivalents is very low by international standards, and the non-employment rate is strikingly high. As in most other European countries, unemployment seems to be largely structural and is concentrated at the lower-end of the labour market and among older people,[25] with an important number of job seekers experiencing very long spells of unemployment.

Labour force and employment

The labour force has grown by over 1 per cent a year on average since 1970, a rate higher than the EC average. It slowed from 1970 to 1977, but it accelerated again in the following period as a result of demographic factors, rising labour force participation rates – in persons – and a pick-up in immigration. While in the 1970s the decline in the male participation rate was broadly offset by the increase in the female participation rate, in the 1980s the former came to an end and the latter accelerated so that the total participation rate rose (Diagram 13, panel A). The female participation rate, which used to be markedly below OECD average levels, has narrowed the gap but among older men (aged 60-64) the participation rate has dropped from about 75 per cent in 1970 to a little over 20 per cent at present – one of the lowest levels in the OECD (Diagram 13, panels B and C). The overall participation rate is about average for EC countries

Diagram 13. **PARTICIPATION RATES**
In persons

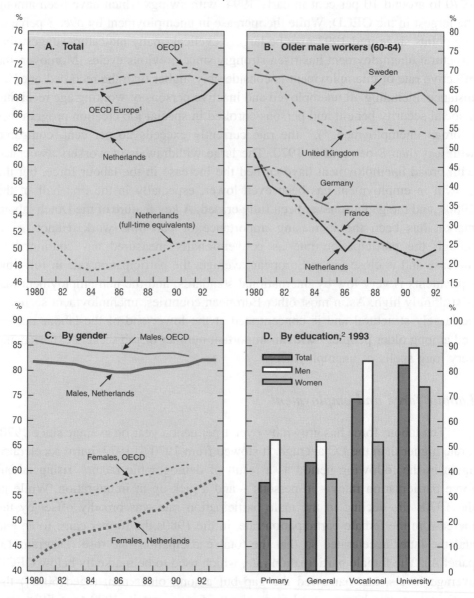

1. Including western Germany before 1991 and total Germany after.
2. National definition.
Sources: Central Bureau of Statistics, Labour Market Survey, 1993 and OECD Secretariat.

but, as most women who entered the labour market in the 1980s took part-time jobs, in full-time equivalents the participation rate is much lower and has remained virtually unchanged over the last two decades (Diagram 13, panel A). Over this whole period, the participation rate, and especially that of older men, has been adversely affected by the rapidly growing number of persons who have entered the disability programme or the early retirement programme, and have thus withdrawn from the labour force (Diagram 14, panel A).[26] For both men and women the participation rate is positively correlated with the education level (Diagram 14, panel B).

More recently, immigration has also contributed to the acceleration of the labour force. Net immigration has increased from an average of 15 000 persons a year in 1981-85 to 35 000 persons in 1986-90. Broadly defined to include asylum-seekers, the number of which has grown very rapidly, immigration seems to have accelerated further in the past couple of years and reached an estimated 60 000 persons in 1993, of 0.4 per cent of total population – a higher percentage than in most other European countries except Germany (Diagram 15). The predominant countries of origin are Turkey, Morocco, Surinam and the Netherlands Antilles. According to official estimates, given the age pattern of recent immigrants (a low proportion of aged and young children) some 60 per cent of them are expected to enter the labour force within a few years: in 1993 this represented some 45 000 persons or about 40 per cent of the increase in the total labour force. Their insertion into the active labour force is a challenge for the Dutch authorities.

In the 1970s and the first half of the 1980s, employment failed to keep up with the growth of the labour force. The period of rapid job creation in the second half of the 1980s was insufficient to close this gap. In full-time equivalents the gap has been sizable (Diagram 14, panel A, and Table 7). However, as over the last decade or so women searching for part-time work have made up the largest part of labour-force entrants, there has been a sustained replacement of full-time by part-time workers in overall employment, and employment has grown appreciably faster in terms of persons than in full-time equivalents. In terms of persons, the performance of the Netherlands has been somewhere between that of the United States and Japan – where a large number of jobs were created – and that of the European Community – with relatively few jobs created (Diagram 14, panel B). On both definitions, employment actually

Diagram 14. OVERVIEW OF THE LABOUR MARKET[1]

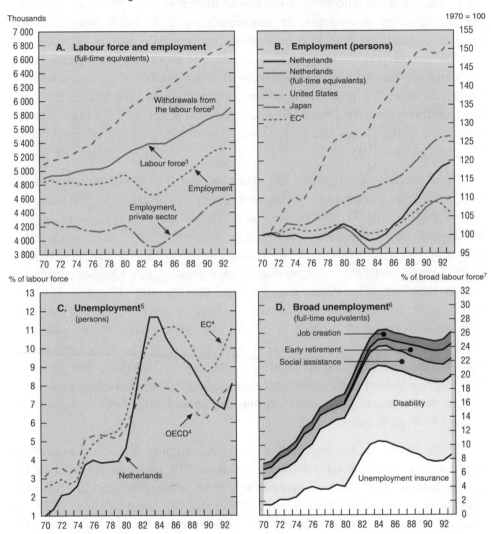

1. 1993 observations are mostly Secretariat estimates.
2. Beneficiaries under disability and early retirement schemes.
3. Total employment and unemployment.
4. Western Germany only.
5. Standardised unemployment.
6. Inactive people of working age receiving social security benefits, and people in job creation programmes.
7. Employment and broad unemployment (excluding job creation).
Sources: Central Planning Bureau, Ministry of Social Affairs and OECD Secretariat.

Diagram 15. **IMMIGRATION[1] IN SELECTED OECD COUNTRIES**

As percentage of population

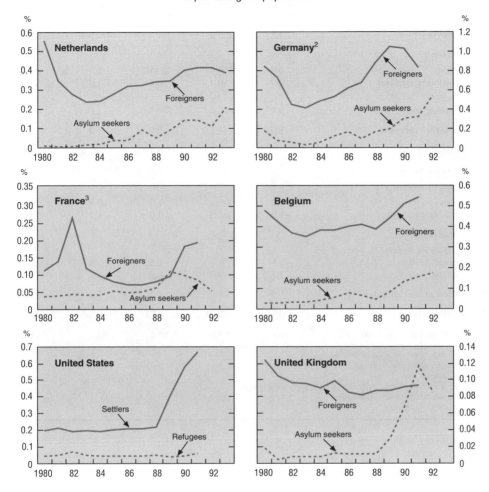

1. "Immigration" is used as a generic term. International comparisons are difficult to make because of differences in definitions and the way migrants are recorded in each country. The United States defines immigrants as those who want to settle whereas European countries generally consider immigrants to be persons of foreign nationality who enter the country and intend to stay for longer than one year. Refugees in the United States refer to lawfully admitted refugees who are allowed to settle, while in Europe asylum seekers include all persons asking for asylum regardless of whether or not they are finally granted this request. All data refer to gross inflows. It is important to bear in mind that outflows, *i.e.* return migration, are significant as well, especially in Europe.
2. Data refer to western Germany up to 1990. As from 1991, data cover Germany as a whole.
3. Break in series in 1990.
Source: OECD, *Trends in International Migration,* SOPEMI, 1993.

59

Table 7. **Economic growth and the labour market**

	1961-73	1974-93	1974-83	1984-91	1992-93[1]
GDP growth[2]	4.8	2.0	1.6	2.9	0.8
Employment[2]					
– persons	0.9	0.9	–0.1	2.1	1.2
– full-time equivalents	0.9	0.5	–0.4	1.6	0.3
of which:					
private sector	0.8	0.4	–0.7	1.9	0.4
Labour force[2] (persons)	1.0	1.2	0.9	1.4	1.7
Unemployment rate[3]	1.1	7.1	5.4	9.2	7.4
Memorandum items:					
Employment intensity[4]					
– persons	–4.0	–1.1	–1.7	–0.8	0.4
– full-time equivalents	–4.0	–1.6	–2.0	–1.3	–0.5
Employment[2]					
(full-time equivalents)					
– exposed sector	–0.5	–0.7	–1.8	0.8	–0.7
– sheltered sector	2.3	0.8	0.0	1.8	1.2
Population of working age[2]	1.5	1.0	1.3	0.8	0.6
Immigration (net)[5]	0.12	0.25	0.21	0.26	0.40
Participation rate (persons)	70.1	65.5	65.1	65.1	68.6

1. 1993 figures are Secretariat estimates.
2. Average annual rate of growth.
3. Standardised rate.
4. Rate of growth of employment less rate of growth of output.
5. As a percentage of total population.
Source: OECD Secretariat.

declined in the 1974-83 period. It rebounded markedly in the subsequent years of strong economic growth, but not sufficiently to catch up with the labour force, and more recently it has weakened again as a result of the cyclical downturn. Both the decline and the rebound in employment were especially pronounced in the private sector. Employment in the public sector increased until the mid-1980s, but since then it has trended down. Over this whole period, the economy has continued its secular shift towards services. While the share of employment in agriculture has edged down and that in industry has declined from

35 in 1975 to 26 per cent in 1992,[27] the share of employment in services has risen to nearly 70 per cent – one of the highest in the OECD.

This aggregate analysis masks strongly divergent trends in different segments of the labour market, notably the dismal performance of the lower end of the market, where job losses have been especially pronounced. Certain low-skilled activities have virtually ceased to exist, in particular in the service sector, where professions such as housekeepers, lift-boys, porters etc. and craftsmen in the construction sector barely exist any longer. Hence, while in 1975 people with only primary education represented 33 per cent of total employment, they represented only 9 per cent in 1993. Since the educational upgrading of the labour force did not keep pace, this trend has been reflected in the growing incidence of low skilled workers in unemployment (see below).

Part-time work, as noted, has become a key feature of the Dutch labour market. Its share in total employment has surged from less than 15 per cent in 1975 to nearly 35 per cent in 1991, a share well above that of any other OECD country (Diagram 16).[28] Part-time jobs mostly concern women – over 60 per cent of female workers hold part-time jobs, the highest proportion in the OECD. But, at nearly 17 per cent, the proportion of men in part-time jobs is also rather important and the highest among OECD countries. More than 65 per cent of part-time workers have a higher education. The growing incidence of part-time work combined with government employment policies and agreements between the social partners aiming at reducing normal working hours[29] has resulted in a fall in the average number of hours a week worked by those in employment to only 33, compared with 39 for the EC as a whole.[30,31] Hence, in the Netherlands, part-time work and the reduction in normal working hours have played an important role in increasing the number of persons actually employed: they have accounted for nearly one half of new jobs created from 1983 to 1991. This trend is likely to continue: recent research by the authorities shows that 10-15 per cent of employees would like to work fewer hours (20-35 hours a week), while 5-10 per cent of employees would like longer work hours. If these wishes were fully satisfied, the mechanical result would be the creation of some 110 000 additional jobs, or 1½ per cent of the labour force.

It is difficult to assess part-time work and determine whether it is a problem since its reasons are not entirely clear. To a large extent, part-time work seems to reflect individual choice – *i.e.* the preferences of both employers and

Diagram 16. **SHARE OF PART-TIME WORKERS IN TOTAL EMPLOYMENT**

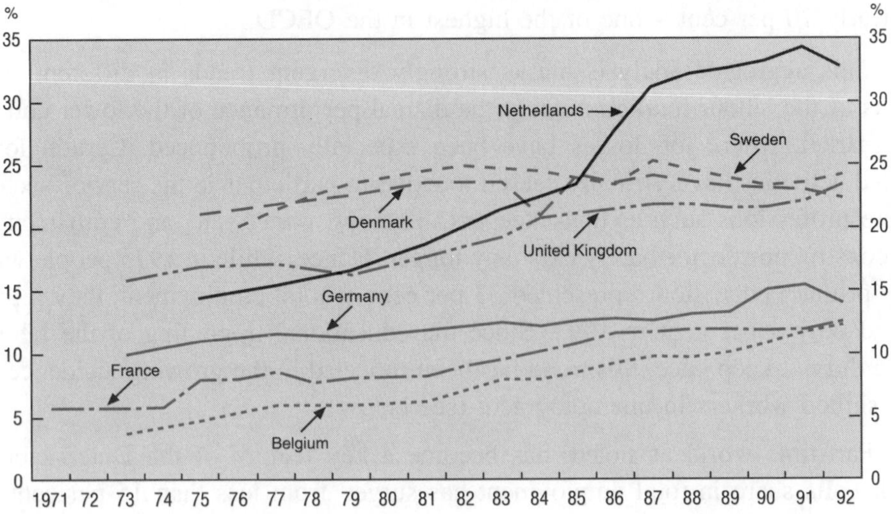

Source: OECD, *Employment Statistics.*

employees – and hence may be seen as an indicator of the flexibility of the Dutch labour market. However, in 1991 over 15 per cent of part-time work was accepted because of the inability to find a full-time job,[32] and a significant proportion of women with part-time jobs may have opted for this solution more because of a lack of day-care facilities for children than for socio-cultural preferences. Also, to a limited extent, part-time work may be the result of distorted incentives, such as social security benefits which would be withdrawn if the recipients were to work more than part-time.

Over the years, the employment content of growth has tended to increase, *i.e.* the rate of growth of the apparent labour productivity of the economy as a whole has declined. In the period 1961-73, the average annual rate of GDP growth was very high (nearly 5 per cent) but the rate of job creation was only around 1 per cent, implying an ''employment intensity of growth'' (*i.e.* the gap between employment and output growth) of around minus 4 percentage points (Table 8). In the 1974-83 period, with slow growth and weak employment, the employment intensity of growth increased: it continued to rise in 1984-91 when

Table 8. Employment, unemployment and non-employment

In full-time equivalents, thousands

	1970	1975	1980	1985	1990	1991	1992	1993[1]
1. Employment[2]	**4 860**	**4 814**	**4 950**	**4 730**	**5 203**	**5 279**	**5 323**	**5 310**
of which:								
Sickness	197	273	306	257	346	346	342	344
2. Broad unemployment[3]	**386**	**689**	**1 031**	**1 700**	**1 730**	**1 740**	**1 770**	**1 862**
Beneficiaries of social security	342	633	957	1 620	1 637	1 644	1 663	1 744
of which:								
Unemployment insurance	76	202	242	666	539	529	541	608
Social assistance	70	118	117	183	180	179	174	172
Early retirement			12	70	128	135	142	149
Disability	196	313	586	701	790	801	806	814
Subsidised employment	44	56	74	80	93	96	107	118
of which:								
Social job creation	44	56	74	80	82	83	85	87
Youth Work Guarantee Plan					7	7	6	11
Job pools					4	6	16	20
3. Inactive people without social security benefits	**2 954**	**3 282**	**3 455**	**3 573**	**3 465**	**3 449**	**3 440**	**3 432**
of which:								
In full-time education	664	923	1 098	1 228	1 144	1 141	1 091	1 091
4. Working age population	**8 156**	**8 728**	**9 362**	**9 923**	**10 305**	**10 372**	**10 434**	**10 494**
5. Broad unemployment rate[4]	**7.4**	**12.6**	**17.4**	**26.8**	**25.3**	**25.1**	**25.3**	**26.4**
6. Non-employment rate[5]	**40.4**	**44.8**	**47.1**	**52.3**	**49.5**	**49.1**	**49.0**	**49.4**

1. Partly based on projections.
2. Including subsidised employment.
3. Inactive people of working age receiving social security benefits and subsidised employment.
4. Broad unemployment as a percentage of broad labour force (*i.e.* employment and broad unemployment, excluding subsidised employment).
5. Broad unemployment (excluding subsidised employment) plus inactive people of working age without social security benefits as a percentage of working age population.

Sources: Ministerie van Sociale Zaken en Werkgelegenheid, Sociale Nota 1994 and Rapportage Arbeidsmarkt 1984 and 1990, Central Bureau of Statistics and Central Planning Bureau.

growth picked up and employment rebounded. Finally, during the current economic slowdown (1992-93), reflecting a poor productivity performance typical of this stage of the cycle, employment intensity has increased further. This long term evolution has been similar but somewhat more accentuated than that experienced by most other European countries and notably the EC. It shows that in the Netherlands, the employment content of growth far from decreasing over time has increased, not only in terms of persons but also in full-time equivalents, possibly reflecting the growing importance of the service sector where productivity levels and gains are lower than in manufacturing.

Unemployment

At less than 1 per cent, unemployment was very low at the beginning of the 1970s. It then rose sharply, especially in the early 1980s, peaking at 11 per cent in 1984. Although it fell significantly in the following period of strong economic expansion, it bottomed at 6.4 per cent in the first half of 1992 – an historically high level, although significantly better than the EC average. During this period, the increase in employment was largely accounted for by new entrants into the labour market, and many unemployed were left in the social security system. More recently, unemployment has been again on a steep uptrend: in early 1994 it exceeded 10 per cent, a level above the OECD average but appreciably below that of most other European countries. These swings in the unemployment rate have been quite large by international standards (Diagram 14, panel C). As it is typically the case in Europe today, Dutch unemployment is characterised by a very uneven incidence across labour force groups, with a high share of low-skilled, female and long-term unemployment (Diagram 17). The rate of unemployment of low skilled workers, *i.e.* workers with only primary education, was over 13 per cent in 1992, more than double the overall rate of unemployment. At nearly 10 per cent, female unemployment is about double that of males, but males are more likely to be long-term unemployed. The relative unemployment rate of older persons has declined rapidly, over the last decade or so, to less than half the average rate, but this has been due to the large inflow of older persons into disability and early retirement programmes. The relative unemployment rate of young workers increased to very high levels a decade ago but, mainly as a consequence of the low number of school-leavers, it has fallen back to the level of 1970s and is currently relatively low by international standards. On the other

Diagram 17. **COMPOSITION OF UNEMPLOYMENT**

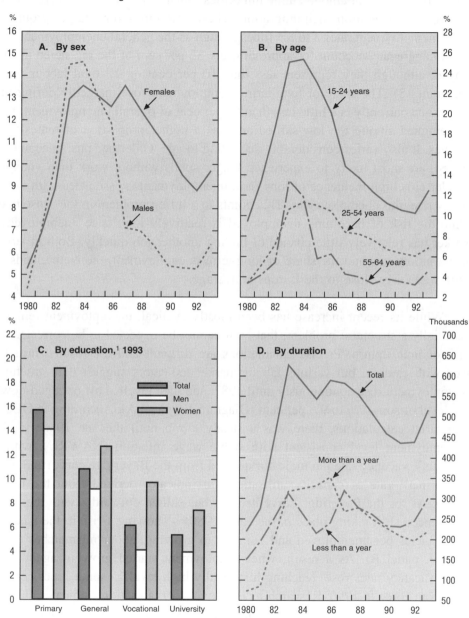

1. National definition.
Sources: Central Bureau of Statistics, Labour Market Survey, 1993 and OECD Secretariat.

hand, unemployment among ethnic minorities remains a problem, exacerbated by the recent acceleration in immigration. These minorities (or "target groups") have unemployment rates 3 to 3.5 times as high as the general unemployment rate and, in aggregate, account for approximately 35 per cent of the registered unemployed, although they represent less than 10 per cent of the total labour force (Diagram 18). The share of long-term unemployment rose markedly during the 1980s, and currently is a little less than 50 per cent of overall unemployment: it is concentrated among the low-skilled and has a higher proportion of males than females. It also varies considerably according to age. Older persons, once unemployed, are most likely to experience longer spells without work than younger people. This high incidence of long-term unemployment is associated with a low inflow rate into unemployment. This points to a hiring problem in the sense that, while the risk of becoming unemployed is relatively low, once unemployed a worker has relatively little chance of finding another job quickly. Both in terms of the inflow rate and the share of long-term unemployment, the Netherlands in 1991 was fairly close to the European average.

While its recent increase has been mostly cyclical, unemployment remains essentially a structural problem, that is, it cannot be expected to be corrected by an economic upturn. Precise calculations are difficult and the results must be used with caution, but various labour market indicators suggest that structural unemployment rose continuously until 1987, and then levelled off or edged-down to a level of some $7^{1}/_{2}$ to $9^{1}/_{2}$ per cent (Diagram 19, panel A). According to OECD Secretariat calculations, there was a steady climb until the late 1980s in the unemployment level consistent with stable wage inflation (NAWRU), with a "normal" vacancy rate (an indicator derived from the Beveridge curve) and with a "normal" rate of capacity utilisation (an indicator derived from the Okun curve). As for the Beveridge curve itself, it has shifted outward – with the most pronounced shift taking place in the early 1980s – showing a rise in the number of vacancies per unemployed and pointing to growing labour mismatches (Diagram 7, panel B). As a result, when employment started growing again after 1984, vacancy rates rose, reaching historically high levels – some 2 per cent of the labour force in 1990. Research by employers' organisations indicates that the number of hidden vacancies could have amounted to 1.5 times the number of regular vacancies, reflecting employers' difficulties in filling the vacancies ("discouraged employers" effect). High numbers of hard-to-fill vacancies have been

Diagram 18. **ETHNIC GROUPS: UNEMPLOYMENT AND PARTICIPATION RATES**

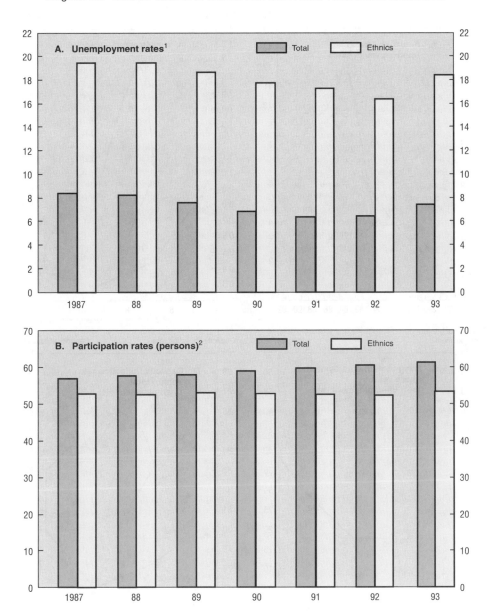

1. National definition ("unemployed labour force").
2. National definition.
Source: Central Bureau of Statistics, Labour Market Survey, 1993.

Diagram 19. **STRUCTURAL ASPECT OF THE LABOUR MARKET**

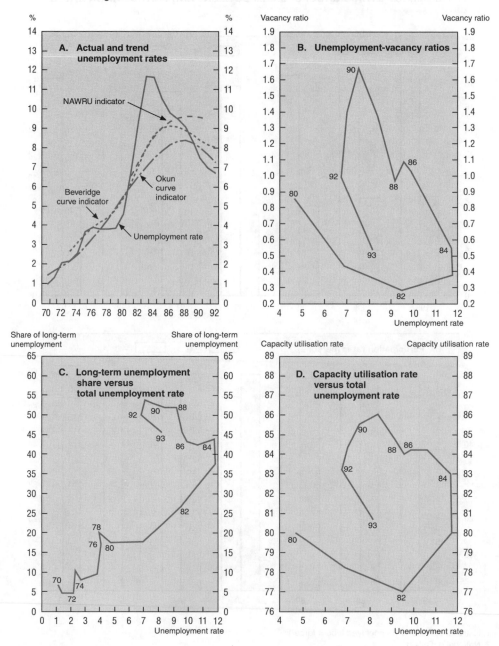

Source: OECD Secretariat.

registered for skilled workers and, until recently, also for unskilled workers despite the high unemployment in this segment of the labour market. Finally, the trend increase in the share of long-term unemployment corroborates the view that unemployment is essentially of a structural character.

As noted in previous Surveys, conventional indicators of unemployment do not fully reflect the degree of slack existing in the Dutch labour market. The unemployment picture looks considerably more distressing on the basis of a broader concept (''broad employment'') including all unemployed and inactive persons of working age receiving a social security benefit and persons enrolled in special job creation programmes. While not all these programmes necessarily represent a form of unemployment, in aggregate they can be seen as providing a broad indicator of the number of people who are not fully employed and receive social benefits or who are in ''subsidized'' employment. On this broad basis, unemployment (in full-time equivalents)[33] has been well above 25 per cent for the last decade (Diagram 14, panel D). Despite the strength of the economy and the rebound in employment in the second half of the 1980s, broad unemployment merely edged down, as a persistent increase in the number of persons receiving disability benefits and enrolled in the early retirement scheme nearly offset the decline in narrow unemployment. On the other hand, the number of persons on social assistance and in job creation programmes was virtually stable. Broad unemployment began rising again in the early 1990s, even before the rebound in narrow unemployment due to the economic downturn. The number of persons receiving a disability benefit and being out of work currently approaches one million, corresponding to nearly 15 per cent of the labour force – a proportion far above that of any other OECD country. Over the years, the disability scheme seems to have been used by both employers and employees as an alternative to unemployment. Estimates of this ''hidden unemployment'' component in the number of disabled persons vary greatly, from a little over 10 per cent to around 50 per cent.

Moreover, broad unemployment does not include: people recorded as unemployed who do not receive social benefits; involuntary part-time work, which as noted seems to be non-negligible, and discouraged workers – *i.e.* workers who either leave the labour force in the face of poor job prospects or decide not to enter. Discouraged workers have been estimated to represent nearly 1 per cent of the labour force.[34] All these factors, and others, are reflected in the non-employment rate (in full-time equivalents) *i.e.* the difference between the population of working age and employment, as a percentage of the former. This rate has in fact increased over time; it is now nearly 50 per cent compared with 47 per cent in 1980 and 40 per cent in 1970 (Table 8). It seems to be extremely high by international standards, although in full-time equivalents the relevant data is not always available.

The high level of broad unemployment has certainly entailed sizeable costs in economic, social and human terms. Its direct budgetary cost has proved exceedingly difficult to reduce: it has been a major obstacle to fiscal consolidation and is largely responsible for the high tax burden which stifles economic activity. As a percentage of GDP, this cost has been edging up again since 1989 and, at around 9 per cent, seems to be markedly higher than in surrounding countries, even though on this point international comparisons are particularly difficult.[35] Its major single component is the cost of disability, which has been stuck at around 4 per cent of GDP for over a decade; the cost of general unemployment insurance is well below its mid-1980s peak of over 4 per cent but still represents some 3 per cent of GDP (Diagram 20). The rise in broad unem-

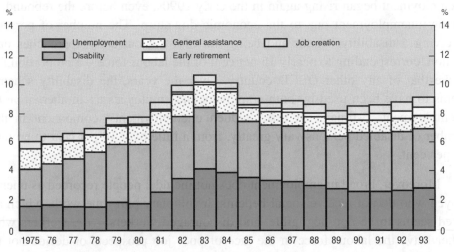

Diagram 20. **THE BUDGETARY COST OF BROAD UNEMPLOYMENT**
In percentage of GDP

Source: Ministry of Social Affairs, Sociale Nota, 1994.

ployment may also account to a considerable extent for the relatively poor performance of the Dutch economy in terms of per capita GDP:[36] an average annual rate of growth of 1.3 per cent from 1980 to 1991, compared with 2.2 per cent for the EC and 1.9 per cent for the OECD, as a whole.

Causes of the problem

It is widely acknowledged that, especially in Europe, unemployment is the result of a variety of complex and often interacting factors which are difficult to disentangle. The Dutch case is no exception to this rule. While the country has been able to react to most of the factors which caused unemployment to reach unprecedented levels in the early 1980s, the adjustment has been only partial and new challenges have now appeared in the global environment. The main causes of the persistence of high unemployment over the cycle seems to have been high labour costs – notably for unskilled labour – reflecting the rigid wage formation system and heavy non-wage costs; insufficient incentives to work resulting from generous social welfare benefits and the tax system; and other rigidities and mismatches in the labour market. At a deeper level, the causes are probably to be found in considerations of social solidarity, equity and fairness which have largely insulated the labour force, especially at the lower-end of the market, from most of the hardship of changing economic conditions. This, in turn, has hindered the adjustment of the economy first, to the wage explosion and the terms-of-trade shocks of the 1970s and, more recently, to the introduction of new technologies, deregulation and globalisation. In today's rapidly integrating world this approach has become more and more economically unsustainable.

High labour costs

When labour costs – *i.e.* wages and employers' social security contributions – are rigid or react slowly to demand and supply shocks they fail in their market-clearing role, and employment bears the brunt of the required adjustment. Hence, labour costs can be seen as a major proximate cause of unemployment. Indeed, in the Netherlands there has been a strong correspondence between, on the one hand, employment and unemployment and, on the other hand, real labour costs and productivity. At the risk of some generalisation, four broad stylised periods can be distinguished:

- In the 1950s and most of the 1960s, on average, real labour costs in the private sector[37] increased less than productivity, unit labour costs declined, the share of wages in national income trended down, the economy grew rapidly and unemployment was very low.
- From the late 1960s until the early 1980s, as a result of the wage explosion and the two oil shocks, inflation accelerated, the economy weakened, and the welfare system was expanded. At first, this expansion could be financed through growing gas revenues but eventually it led to a marked increase in the tax burden and to a sort of vicious circle – which came to be called the "Dutch disease". Real labour costs increased sharply, exceeding productivity gains: the profit position and the international competitiveness of enterprises deteriorated, real invest-ment and net exports (excluding natural gas) collapsed, and the economy finally went into a pronounced recession (1981-82). Labour-intensive industries – such as shipbuilding, mining and textiles – were progres-sively phased out or shifted abroad to low labour cost countries. How-ever, for a while, the impact of rising real labour costs on private sector employment was cushioned by government regulations, the attitude of the unions and, possibly, recollections of persistent labour scarcity. It was not until the early 1980s that the long-delayed labour shake-out took place, especially in the exposed manufacturing sector: it led to a surge in the unemployment rate but also to strong productivity gains which began to reduce the share of wages in national income and alleviate the profit squeeze (Table 9 and Diagram 21).
- From 1983 until 1990, the economy first recovered and then grew strongly. The period was marked by a major reorientation of economic policy away from demand management towards a more market-oriented approach and fiscal consolidation. This and wage moderation were the cornerstones of the recovery. Real labour costs edged-down, real unit labour costs fell sharply and the share of wages moved back to the levels of the late 1960s. The improved profit situation and better international competitiveness resulted in an investment boom and strong economic growth. Unemployment declined rapidly, but again with a noticeable lag with respect to the evolution of labour costs.
- Since 1990, and until very recently, the growth of labour costs, in nominal as well as in real terms, has accelerated again, leading to a

72

Table 9. **Labour costs and productivity**

	1971-84			1985-89			1990-93			1971-93		
	A	B	C	A	B	C	A	B	C	A	B	C
	Average annual rates of change											
1. Netherlands[1]	2.7	2.9	–0.1	–0.3	1.2	–1.5	2.1	0.9	1.2	2.0	2.2	–0.2
of which:												
Exposed sector	4.8	4.7	0.0	–0.2	1.8	–2.0	4.3	2.1	2.1	3.6	3.6	–0.0
2. OECD Europe[2]	3.1	2.9	0.2	1.3	2.4	–1.2	1.7	1.9	–0.2	2.4	2.6	–0.2
3. OECD Total[2]	2.8	2.6	0.2	1.2	2.2	–0.9	1.6	1.7	–0.1	2.2	2.4	–0.1

	1984			1989			1993		
	A	B	C	A	B	C	A	B	C
	Cumulated change since 1970								
1. Netherlands[1]	145.5	148.8	97.8	143.3	157.7	90.9	155.5	163.1	95.3
of which:									
Exposed sector	191.5	190.6	100.5	186.8	207.3	90.1	223.8	226.3	98.9
2. OECD Europe[2]	152.6	148.8	103.0	162.6	168.3	97.1	174.4	181.8	96.3
3. OECD Total[2]	147.1	144.1	102.1	156.7	161.1	97.5	167.9	172.7	97.2

A = Real labour costs.
B = Labour productivity.
C = Real unit labour costs.

1. Excluding mining and quarrying.
2. Excluding Norway and United Kingdom, western Germany only.
Source: OECD Secretariat.

sizeable increase in unit labour costs and a new upward trend in the share of wages. At the same time, mainly reflecting developments in surrounding countries, the economy has moved into a cyclical downturn. After a period of labour hoarding which lasted until mid-1992, especially in manufacturing, down-sizing and lay-offs have been widespread, the unemployment rate has rebounded, following real unit labour costs with a shorter lag than in the 1970s.

It is especially at the lower end of the market that wages have failed in their market-clearing role. There, employment dropped markedly in the second half of

Diagram 21. **LABOUR COST,[1] WAGE SHARE AND UNEMPLOYMENT**

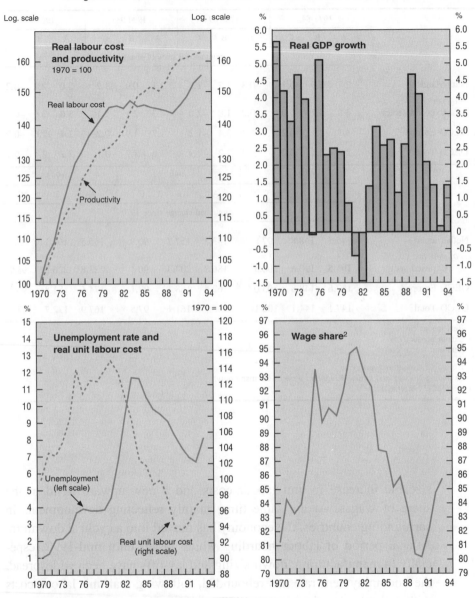

1. Business sector excluding mining and quarrying.
2. Central Planning Bureau definition, business sector exluding mining and quarrying.
Sources: Central Planning Bureau and OECD Secretariat.

the 1970s and the first years of the 1980s, a development which was much more pronounced than in surrounding countries and may have reflected the then excessive level of the legal minimum wage. Despite an unemployment rate about double the overall rate and a reduction and freeze of the legal minimum wage over the last decade or so, real wages of low paid workers have continued to grow, and virtually as fast as the private sector average (Diagram 22, panels B and C). As a result, the strong decline in the demand for unskilled labour relative to skilled labour has not been accompanied by any significant widening of the wage structure (Diagram 22, panel D). This has been in sharp contrast with the evolution in a few other OECD countries, and notably the United States, where real wages at the lower end of the market have actually fallen and the wage structure has widened (Diagram 22, panel B). In 1990, among OECD countries, only Denmark had a lower ratio of the average wage to the minimum wage. In the United States, this ratio was 2½ times that of the Netherlands.[38] Hence, the lower end of the Dutch wage structure looks compressed by international standards, and points to labour-market rigidities.[39]

Confronted with excessive labour costs, enterprises have responded by substituting capital for labour – the predictable reaction in a small, open economy with a strong currency policy where many price increases are limited by international competition. Wage moderation in the 1980s helped a lot but, given the persistently high tax burden, it was not sufficient. Capital intensity unambiguously rose over 1973-85 when the increase in the stock of capital was accompanied by an actual decline in employment (Diagram 23). This was reflected in a shift in the relationship between unemployment and capacity utilisation, or Okun-curve (Diagram 19, panel B). Since the mid-1980s and until very recently, with a declining price of labour relative to the price of capital (Diagram 24), employment grew in tandem with the capital stock, suggesting that investment, which had been essentially capital deepening, became more capital widening. In this respect, however, there has been a sharp dichotomy between the exposed sector and the sheltered sector of the economy. In the exposed sector, over 1970-92, production nearly doubled and employment contracted by over 15 per cent (in full-time equivalents). On the other hand, in the sheltered sector, with a smaller increase in production, employment rose by 20 per cent. But even in the exposed sector during the period of wage moderation the dominant trend was reversed,

Diagram 22. LOWER END OF THE LABOUR MARKET

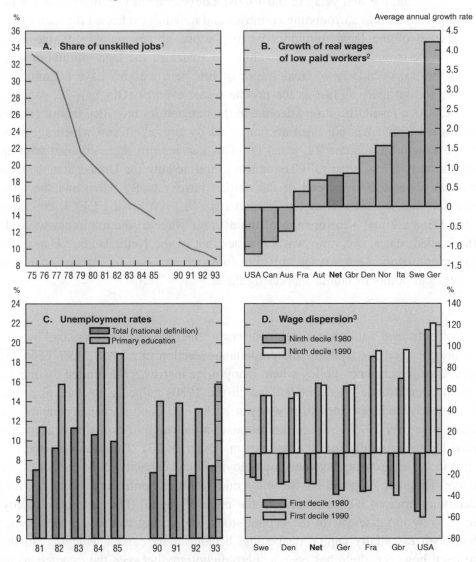

1. Per cent of workers with only primary education in total employment.
2. The earnings definition is gross hourly earnings of all workers, where available: Denmark, France, Netherlands, Norway, Sweden, the United Kingdom and the United States.
   1980-87: France and Italy; 1980-89: United States; 1980-90: Denmark; 1980-91: Australia, Austria, Netherlands and Norway; 1980-92: United Kingdom; 1981-90: Canada; 1981-91: Sweden; 1983-88: Germany.
3. Wage difference in per cent of medium.
Sources: Central Bureau of Statistics, Labour Market Survey, 1992 and 1993 and OECD Secretariat.

Diagram 23. **GROSS FIXED CAPITAL STOCK AND EMPLOYMENT**

1973-93, business sector, volume indices, 1973 = 100

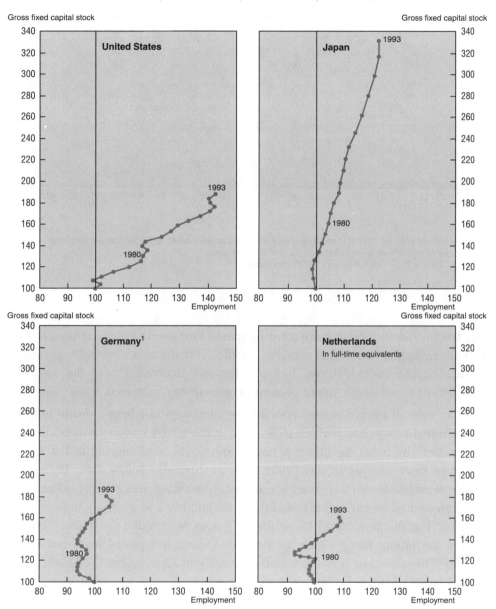

1. Western Germany only.
Source: OECD Secretariat.

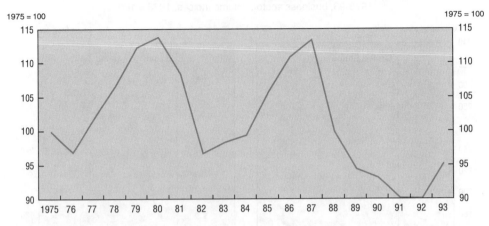

Diagram 24. **RELATIVE FACTOR PRICES**[1]

1975 = 100   1975 = 100

1. Series derived from the Central Planning Bureau F.K. model; series defined as labour cost per employee
   (adjusted for productivity growth) divided by a cost of capital index.
Sources: Central Planning Bureau and OECD Secretariat.

and from 1984 to 1991 employment increased along with output (Diagram 25). Perhaps reflecting the shift to services, for the economy as a whole, the growth of productivity, as noted above, has continuously decreased over the last two decades – *i.e.* the employment content of growth has increased.

As a result of widespread restructuring and capital-labour substitution, the surge in real labour costs which took place in the 1970s was more than matched by productivity gains, so that real unit labour costs, after surging in the 1970s, fell even more sharply in the 1980s, and are currently below their 1970 level (Table 9 and Diagram 21, panel C). Hence, firms have successfully adjusted to the high cost of labour and restored their profitability and international competitiveness. But this new broad "equilibrium" does not entail a satisfactory utilisation of the labour force which, to a certain extent, has priced itself out of the market. This situation is not unusual, especially in Europe, but the Dutch economy seems to have gone further than most others towards a state of high labour cost/high productivity/high non-employment. While high wages were the initial cause, owing to the subsequent increase in unemployment nowadays non-wage contributions – mainly to support inactive persons – are mainly responsible for

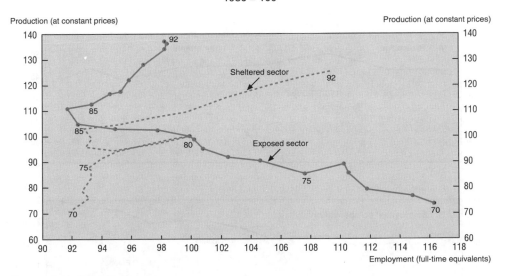

Diagram 25. **PRODUCTION AND EMPLOYMENT**
1980 = 100

Source: Central Planning Bureau.

high labour costs. Indeed, real take-home pay is about average by international standards, but the tax-wedge – at nearly 45 per cent – is strikingly higher than the European and the OECD average (Diagram 26).[40] In fact, the welfare system has greatly slowed the adjustment of labour costs, which underlines the strong inter-relation between unemployment, welfare assistance and the tax burden. In other words, the vicious circle set in motion by the "Dutch disease" in the 1970s has been stopped, but it has not been fully reversed. Its roots are in the lower-end of the labour market where rigidities, disincentives and unemployment are especially high. But because of the social security contributions needed to support these unemployed persons, this sectoral problem leads to higher labour costs in the whole economy, jeopardising employment at all levels – although it is once again unskilled workers who are the most threatened due to their poor productivity.

High and inflexible labour costs may be especially detrimental for employment to the extent that the present environment is marked by accelerated techno-logical change and heightened global competition. Technological evolution is

Diagram 26. TAX WEDGE, EMPLOYEE'S COMPENSATION AND TAKE-HOME PAY OF AN AVERAGE PRODUCTION WORKER

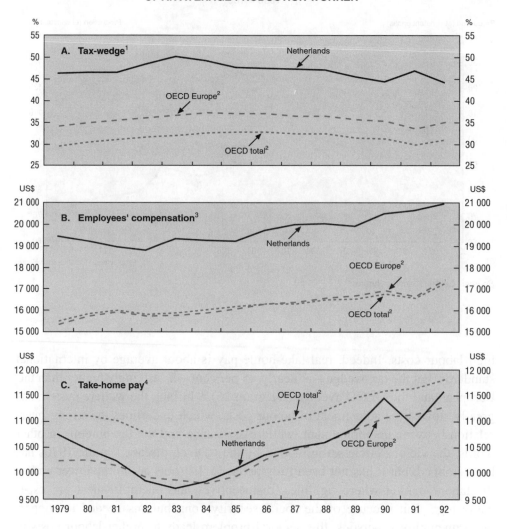

1. Tax wedge is defined as the ratio of tax plus employee's and employer's contributions over total employee's compensation.
2. Excluding Portugal, Greece, Iceland, Luxembourg, Turkey.
3. Deflated by GDP price index (1985 = 1) and converted to US$ using 1985 purchasing power parities.
4. Deflated by private consumption price index (1985 = 1) and converted to US$ using 1985 purchasing power parities.
Sources: OECD, The Tax Benefit Position of Production Workers, 1979-1992, and OECD Secretariat estimates.

nothing new of course, but the pace of change may have greatly accelerated, especially in the field of information technology. Past experience suggests that this can be expected to result in higher standards of living. But how fast and how smoothly it will happen depends on the ability of countries to adapt and exploit the potential of these new technologies in terms of new activities, jobs and products. Although this point can hardly be quantified, the little analysis available indicates that in the United States technological change has markedly reduced the demand for unskilled labour; and anecdotal evidence suggests that this may also have been the case in the Netherlands.

International competition also seems to have recorded a quantum change over the past few years and one aspect of it – "globalisation", *i.e.* the transfer of production to low-wage countries – is now at the centre of attention, especially concerning its impact on wages and employment. Globalisation is the result of several elements: the liberalisation and deregulation of financial markets and international capital movements; new information technologies; and, perhaps most important, the sudden collapse of communism and the adoption by many countries outside the OECD area of an outward-looking market approach. Hence, major new players have appeared on the global market which, for an advanced economy like the Dutch one, not only represent additional competitors and clients, but also offer the possibility of cutting costs by shifting production there. Virtually all manufacturing sectors may be concerned, as well as a range of services such as wholesale and retail trade, transport and communications, finance and personal services. However, due to a lack of timeliness and other problems with the data, it is still impossible to assess its implications for employment in the Netherlands.

The tentative conclusion of work done in the OECD Secretariat[41] is that globalisation has decreased the demand for unskilled workers in OECD countries and increased that for skilled workers. But, until recently at least, these effects have been relatively small, with no clear implications for overall employment. Nonetheless, this sectoral shift in the demand for labour has accentuated a similar and more pronounced shift caused by technical progress noted above, and has aggravated the plight of unskilled workers. Moreover, mounting anecdotal evidence suggests that the pace of globalisation may have accelerated in the more recent period not yet covered by the data, and several other considerations lend support to the view that the potential effect on the labour market of OECD countries could soon be more significant. These considerations include: the sheer size of the cheap labour force now available outside the OECD area, which could considerably extend the time needed for economic growth there to narrow the wage gap; the fact that this labour force is relatively well-educated and/or well disciplined; and, perhaps more important, that globalisation often includes a transfer of technology which leads to a combination of state-of-the-art factories and managerial skills with low-cost labour. This is especially the case when the shift of production to low-wage countries is the result of direct investment and joint ventures. Indeed, the Dutch authorities view globalisation as representing additional competition not only for the lower end of the labour market but, in many cases, also for relatively skilled labour.[42]

This being said, the threat that globalisation might lead to some degree of industrial decline in an advanced economy like the Dutch one, bringing unemployment in its wake, should not be overstated. Distance and political risk still play an important role when deciding on the location of production. As a few well advertised cases have recently shown, important but acceptable concessions on wages and other labour costs may tilt the balance in favour of keeping production at home.[43] Hence, substantial labour-cost differentials are not necessarily unbeatable provided reasonable steps are taken to improve the flexibility of the domestic labour market. More importantly, globalisation also implies the emergence of new market opportunities, and the Netherlands would seem well positioned to exploit them, given its long historical tradition of trading, its very open and outward looking economy, and a few multinational corporations which have been engaged in this process for decades already. On the other hand, over 80 per cent of Dutch foreign trade is with Europe, and reflecting specialisation in rather low-tech and medium-tech goods – such as food and traditional chemical products – and a relatively low share of capital goods and R&D intensive industries, less than 20 per cent of exports are accounted for by capital goods – which are the type of goods low-wage countries currently need most. Also, Dutch firms may not have been sufficiently dynamic and innovative in recent years, in part due to the web of restrictive agreements, regulations and barriers to entry which have characterised many sectors of the economy. According to provisional figures, Dutch exports to Eastern Europe and Southeast Asia[44] recorded two-digit rates of growth last year: but so did imports from these areas and the fairly large trade deficit *vis-à-vis* Southeast Asia widened again. Hence, further efforts are needed if the Netherlands is to offer low-wage economies the right mix of goods, at competitive prices, and with the backing of sufficient support and financing arrangements, as required by today's trade.

Impediments to wage flexibility and the welfare system

The reasons why wages have not shown more flexibility in the face of persistent unemployment seem to be institutional, legal and contractual, *i.e.* the wage formation system, the administrative extension of sectoral wage agreements and the minimum wage combined with the generous welfare system and the tax structure. Altogether, these elements have effectively prevented or discouraged the unemployed ("outsiders") from bidding for lower wages. As for the persistently high level of non-wage labour costs, this reflects the importance of welfare spending.

Empirical evidence suggests that in the Netherlands the lay-off rate or the change in unemployment level have stronger downward effects on wages than the level of unemployment.[45] The level of unemployment itself does not have a significant impact. As for long-term unemployment, it does not exert much downward pressure on wages in any case.[46] These findings imply that the "insider-outsider" theory may have some validity as an explanation of the high incidence of long-term unemployment and the slow adjustment of real wages. Since the early 1980s, wage negotiations have been taking place at the sectoral level – a wage formation process which can be considered as an intermediate case between a centralised one and one at the firm level. Through an automatic legal extension, wage agreements between unions and employers cover the whole sector concerned, despite sharply reduced rates of unionisation. These agreements have tended to raise wages at the bottom end of the wage scale more than proportionately – often outweighing opposite forces arising from market conditions – and hence reduce wage dispersion. Moreover, administrative extension decreases the responsiveness of wages to labour market conditions at the micro level and is an effective barrier to the entry of new enterprises, as new firms' ability to compete on the basis of labour costs is reduced. In a paper recently submitted to Parliament, the Government has compared the wage levels in sectors covered by an extended collective labour agreement with the wage level in other sectors and estimated at 3 per cent the increase in levels due to the automatic extension. For low wages, this increase in levels was estimated to be 12-15 per cent.

A high legal minimum wage relative to the productivity of unskilled workers may also have significantly impaired the clearing process in the labour market. Until the early-1980s, the level of the legal minimum wage was nearly 70 per cent that of the average wage – an extremely high level by international standards. In 1984 the legal minimum wage was lowered and then frozen in nominal terms for several years, a measure which had a clearly positive effect on employment.[47] At the same time however, as the growth of minimum wages in collective agreement tended to follow the agreed average wage growth, the gap between the legal minimum wage and the minimum wage in collective agreements progressively increased. In many sectors the effective lowest wage is now considerably higher than the legally required minimum wage, and on average this gap is about 12 per cent (see Diagram 27). Moreover, the difference between the actual average hourly wage of adult employees at the lowest end of the labour market and the lowest salary scales in collective labour agreements is about 8 per cent, so that actual wages in this segment of the market are about 20 per cent above the legal minimum wage. Also, the number of workers at the legal minimum wage has steadily declined and currently represents less than 3 per cent of the total. The (gross) legal minimum wage is now a little over 60 per cent of the average wage.

The generosity of welfare programmes – in terms of eligibility and benefits – has affected labour costs in several ways. Because of their budgetary cost, these programmes have increased social security contributions and the tax wedge, thereby adding to labour costs directly and, as wages are largely negotiated on an after-tax basis, also indirectly. Even more importantly, unemployment and other welfare programmes by reducing the financial incentive to find a job, seem to have encouraged unemployment[48] and decreased downward pressure on real wages, especially at the lower end of the market. Hence, combined with the automatic administrative extension of sectoral wage agreements, high reservation wages may have been the main reason for the development and persistence of an important gap between actual minimum wages and the legal minimum wage.

As discussed in the previous Survey and briefly reviewed below, despite a decade of efforts to redress the mix between ''active'' and ''passive'' measures, labour-market policy remains characterised by generous income-support mea-

Diagram 27. **RELEVANCE OF LEGAL MINIMUM WAGE**

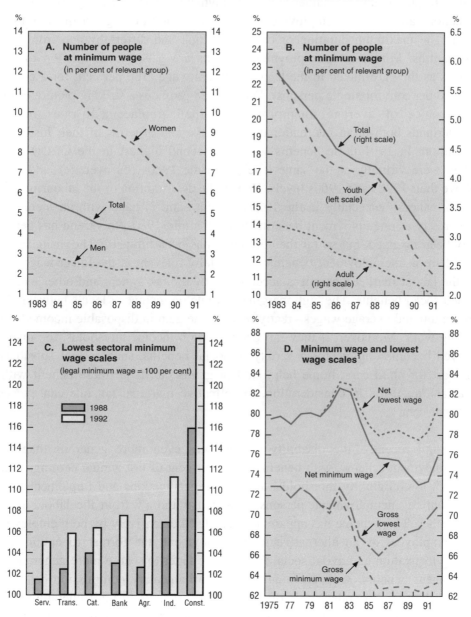

1. As a percentage of average-production-worker wage, including child allowances.
Sources: Central Planning Bureau; Central Bureau of Statistics and Ministry of Finance, Budget 1994.

sures. Replacement rates under the unemployment scheme for all types of family situations and for all unemployment spells are among the highest in the OECD area. The maximum duration of benefits is long and differs by age from 9 to 60 months. Minimum unemployment benefits are generous in relation to low wages as they are linked to the legal minimum wage (100 per cent for a couple and 70 per cent for single persons). Diagram 28 provides a striking picture of the importance of average unemployment benefit replacement rates in the Netherlands both in an international perspective and in terms of their historical evolution. In 1991 these benefits were the second highest in the OECD area. They were virtually at the same level as in the 1980s (on average), and well above their 1970s and 1960s levels. Hence, the deterioration of the labour market performance – especially in the 1970s – went hand in hand with an increased generosity of unemployment benefits. Since the mid-1980s, this trend has generally been reversed, but so far the correction has been limited.[49] The disincentive problem of unemployment benefits is especially relevant at the lower-wage end of the labour market where it is accentuated by the tax system and other means-tested social benefits. The high marginal tax rate on income at levels between the minimum and average wages greatly reduces the gain in disposable income from taking work. Moreover, if they fall below certain income thresholds, the unemployed become eligible for a variety of social benefits, such as rent subsidies, support for child care, home help, student grants etc. If all these benefit withdrawals are taken in consideration, the effective marginal tax rate can exceed 100 per cent.[50]

Until recently, the disability scheme was even more generous than the unemployment scheme, with benefits of 70 per cent of last annual earnings until age 65, low eligibility thresholds, and loose specifications and implementation: and, unlike unemployment, persons joining it withdraw from the labour force altogether. This scheme has apparently been used extensively by both employers and employees as an alternative to unemployment: the former to circumvent hiring legislation and avoid social friction; the latter to secure more generous or permanent benefits. A recent inquiry by a parliamentary commission has confirmed that an "extended use" of the disability scheme to limit unemployment was tolerated by the authorities until 1987 (and hence did not represent an outright "abuse").[51] However, the commission did not quantify this extended use. Since 1987, the Government has been trying to tighten the disability scheme

Diagram 28. **UNEMPLOYMENT BENEFIT REPLACEMENT RATES SINCE THE 1960s**[1]

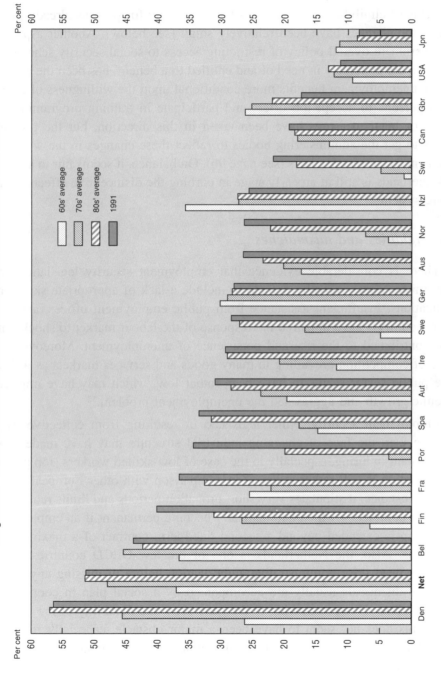

1. Benefits before tax as a percentage of previous earnings before tax. Countries are ranked in descending order of replacement rates in 1991.
Source: OECD Secretariat.

– in terms of eligibility and benefits – but, especially for persons already in the scheme, the changes have been relatively small (see below). Another aspect of the Government overall policy of restricting access to social security schemes to those who are genuinely in need of and entitled to a benefit, has been the attempt to make unemployment benefits more conditional upon the willingness of unemployed persons to accept job offers and participate in training programmes. A number of legal measures have been taken in this direction, but the problem remains to get the administering bodies to reflect these changes in the way they implement social security laws (see page 96). On balance, it seems fair to say that the Netherlands is still at an early stage in curbing the disincentive effects of the welfare system.

Other rigidities and mismatches

There is considerable evidence that employment security legislation and labour mismatches – broadly defined to include a lack of appropriate skills and qualifications, insufficient assistance from public employment offices, and low labour mobility – have impaired the response of the labour market to shocks and hence contributed to the rise and persistence of unemployment. Moreover, the degree of competition prevailing in many goods and services markets as well as in the public sector seems to have been rather low, which may have impaired economic growth and aggravated the unemployment problem.[52]

Employment security, either legislated or resulting from collective wage agreements, in the face of changing industrial structure may have made firms more hesitant in hiring, especially in the case of low-skilled workers. Job protection legislation is still rather stringent in comparison with other European countries. For instance, it stipulates very short probation periods and limits renewal of temporary contracts – which automatically become permanent if an employment relationship is extended beyond a second fixed-term contract of a maximum of six months. Also, the Netherlands is one of the few OECD countries where employers need prior administrative authorization before dismissing any workers. Large dismissals usually are accompanied by a social plan in cooperation with the unions. However, owing to the generosity and flexibility of the welfare system, this does not seem to have been a major obstacle, especially for large firms. Moreover, to circumvent these rules, employers have made extensive use of fixed-term contracts – typically for one year. Although most of the people with a fixed-term contract eventually acquire permanent status, these contracts are perceived by employers as a useful screening device at the time of first hire. Even more spectacular has been the increase in the use of temporary employment from job agencies. The number of hours of work supplied by the 1 220 temporary employment agencies has tripled between 1983 and 1991,[53] when over 2 per cent of all dependent workers were employed via one of these agencies – the highest share reported from any OECD country. On a broad definition, these agencies may account for more than half of all hirings.[54] Research carried out by the authorities suggests that the possibility of finding a job through fixed-term contracts and temporary employment agencies has been used mainly by young unemployed and women reentering the labour market; and that people with a temporary work contract, by and large, do want this kind of arrangement and carry out work which is temporary – such as a temporary extension of a firm's workload or replacement of absent staff. Finally, it should be noted that one of the aims of employment protection legislation and job security negotiated by collective agreements is to reduce the rate of labour turnover, encourage investment in on-the-job training, and hence reduce labour resistance to change.

On balance, employment protection legislation seems to have been detrimental to employment. For instance, the OECD Secretariat has found that for the Netherlands this legislation – in terms of dismissal costs and notice period – makes a higher estimated contribution to long-term unemployment than other labour-market policy variables such as the maximum duration of unemployment benefits and the ratio of active programme expenditure to unemployment benefits.[55] This applies to blue-collar as well as white-collar workers. Moreover, employment from job agencies is costly, since employers must pay these agencies for the services they provide. Without the rigidities related to job protection legislation, some of the resources absorbed by the temporary employment agencies would be available for a more productive use. Finally, job protection and lags in obtaining the administrative permission for dismissals or the agreement of the unions may help explain that, as noted, the reaction of unemployment to the recent downturn has been more delayed and ultimately sharper than in other European countries.

Important labour-market mismatches began to be noticed in the mid-1980s, when employment started rising again. The Beveridge curve – that is, the number of vacancies per unemployed – showed a pronounced outward shift in 1983-84, and this trend broadly continued until 1989, reaching unprecedented levels. Since then, reflecting the economic downturn, the Beveridge curve has shifted inward, and the vacancy rate has declined markedly but, until recently at least, the vacancy rate and the share of vacancies that are difficult to fill have remained important for persons with low skills and qualifications, suggesting that mismatches continue to be significant and are concentrated in this segment of the labour market. Mismatches may result from a variety of factors. The education system – broadly defined to include apprenticeship training – and its capacity to provide skills and qualifications in line with what is required by the market place was a major issue in the Netherlands in the 1980s, and many criticisms were expressed. As a result, improvements have already taken place. The participation in secondary vocational education has nearly doubled over the last ten years or so, and the social partners are now sharing with the government the responsibility of determining the content and quality of vocational training, the final decision being taken by the Minister for Education and Science. The proportion of upper secondary students in vocational education (including apprenticeship) is about average by European standards, but is above the OECD average. The situation is similar for the percentage of 18-year-olds enrolled in education (nearly 75 per cent in 1991). Nonetheless, problems remain. The unemployment of school leavers is on the rise again (from 15 per cent in 1990 to 20 per cent in 1992); still too many young people enter the labour market without a minimal qualification (15 000 drop-outs a year); there are too many persons with a higher education in the social sciences and the literary field compared with the market requirements; and the number of persons entering in apprenticeship training, after increasing for years, has begun to decline again, partly because too many of the young unemployed are not sufficiently qualified to enrol in existing programmes. Of these problems, that of the drop-outs seems especially worrisome. More generally, however, like most other OECD countries, the Netherlands seems to be faced with a school-to-work problem.

Since in the Netherlands financial incentives for active job search by the unemployed are particularly weak, there is considerable scope for other ways of enhancing active labour market participation – for instance through contacts between persons without work and the benefit and employment administration. These contacts may take the form of signing-on, in-depth interviews, offers of job vacancies and offers of places in job-creation or retraining programmes. In the absence of such "active" measures, especially the low qualified unemployed risk being caught in a negative spiral of rejection and stigmatisation, which greatly reduces their chances of finding a job. Until recently, the performance of the Dutch Public Employment Service (PES) seemed rather mediocre, notably with respect to its ability of offering job vacancies. For example, in 1990, the average interval between two vacancy offers by the public employment service to an unemployed person amounted to as much as 16 months – the fourth longest span in the European OECD area.[56] As discussed below, in 1990 the PES was reorganised with a view to improve its effectiveness in employment-finding and reducing mismatches in local labour markets. However, this reorganisation seems unlikely to increase the pressure on the unemployed to pursue an active job search since the imposition of sanctions when benefit claimants fail to accept jobs or retraining was not included in the tripartite decision-making process of the PES and was left with the Industrial Insurance Boards[57] and municipalities. Cooperation between the PES, on one side, and the Industrial Insurance Boards and the Municipalities, on the other, has been insufficient. Although it has improved in recent years, further progress is necessary.

Looking at "active" labour-market policies as a whole – i.e. policies aiming at improving access to the labour market, job-related skills and labour market functioning – the Netherlands has been broadly in line with the OECD average in terms of expenditures as a percentage of GDP (0.4 in 1990, compared with 0.3 in 1985); but it was the country with the lowest expenditures on "active" programmes as a percentage of total labour market expenditures (around 15 per cent, compared with 10 per cent in 1985).[58] Since 1990, the authorities have taken further steps to redress the mix between "active" and "passive" policies: these have included the "Labour pools", the "route placement" and the Youth Work Guarantee Plan (see next section). Also, special counselling and guidance for ethnic minorities have been substantially increased. But in view of the size of the problem, the authorities feel that much remains to be done in this area.

Finally, labour mobility may have been hampered – and hence, mismatches aggravated – by the strong reliance on social housing, entry regulations to municipal housing markets, and features of the pension system. Compared with other OECD countries, the regulated housing and rental sector is much larger in the Netherlands, where 98 per cent of rented dwellings are subject to price regulation and quantity rationing. As the rents in this sector are below the market price and because of uncertainties concerning the availability of social housing in other regions, with the risk of having to queue again, people may be discouraged from accepting jobs in different regions. To some extent, however, these considerations may be offset by the fact that a large part of the country is typically within commuting distance. As for pension schemes, in the Netherlands the volume of built-up rights cannot always be fully transferred when moving to a new job, a rigidity which may have been another obstacle to labour mobility. However, in recent years, considerable progress has been made in this area, and the non-transferability of pension rights may currently affect only about 10 per cent of the labour force.

Labour-market policies

How the approach has changed

The focus of Dutch labour-market policy has shifted considerably over the last two decades or so; first, in the direction of income-support measures as the authorities, like those in most other European countries, reacted to the shocks and economic difficulties of the 1970s by strengthening the welfare system in an effort to cushion the standard of living of workers losing their jobs; and then, as the harmful economic effects and unsustainability of this approach became progressively evident, towards more "active" policies and stronger incentives to work. The still unbalanced mix of "active" and "passive" programmes noted above, reflects both the high level of benefits and the large number of beneficiaries, and is largely the heritage of past developments. It is especially hard to redress it in the current environment of rising unemployment – which inflates expenditures on "passive" programmes – and fiscal consolidation – which limits the possibility of increasing expenditure on "active" programmes. Finally, it must be noted that since the early 1980s, wage moderation has been, in the view of the authorities, an essential complement to all labour-market policies.

The objectives of "active" policies have changed markedly. In the early 1970s, "active" labour measures were mainly focused on the demand side, and particularly on job creation with public support in labour-intensive sectors such as public infrastructures or construction and on job protection through subsidies to firms in financial difficulty. From the late 1970s, these policies were significantly reduced and both of them were abandoned by the mid-1980s. "Active" labour-market programmes, which have gained momentum in the past few years, are now aiming at reducing long-term unemployment by improving access to the labour market and job-related skills. The "Labour pools", introduced in 1990, are targeted to specific groups with high unemployment rates and a low chance of getting a new job through the regular functioning of the labour market. The so-called "route placement" introduced in the early 1990s provides a plan tailored to the characteristics and needs of the long-term unemployed, ranging from remotivation, to training or retraining, to work experience and to placement in the open labour market. Such an approach, which has also been introduced in other countries, seeks to make the most effective use of the diversity of training possibilities in the Netherlands. The Youth Work Guarantee Plan became operational nationwide at the beginning of 1992 to address the problem of youth unemployment. It offers youngsters a combination of training and work experience, the ultimate goal being the transition to a permanent job. The target group consists of all persons unemployed for at least 6 months and aged up to 21 and all unemployed school leavers up to the age of 27. Young immigrants and asylum seekers will also be allowed to participate. The aim of the authorities is to increase the number of participants from around 7 000 in late 1993 – representing less than 10 per cent of total youth unemployed – to some 10 000 in 1996; and by 1998, all unemployed youth in this target group should participate. In 1992, participation was restricted to members of the target group up to the age of 18 and 21, respectively. The age level will be raised progressively each year. This growth path has been determined by the expected number of suitable jobs available and the effectiveness of other measures to facilitate youth employment. Recently this Plan has been complemented by a new programme to train those youngsters who are not prepared to move directly to a work experience. There are still no official comprehensive assessments of "route placement" and the Youth Work Guarantee Plan. The authorities feel that the effects have been positive although they have been swamped by the recent deterioration of labour-market conditions which has caused unemployment, even among young persons, to increase steeply.

Along with the above initiatives, the authorities have tried to reduce the generosity of income-support measures in order to redress the incentive balance between working and not working, curb the cost of these programmes and hence reduce non-wage labour cost. However, the results, on balance, have been modest. One approach has been to curb the link between the level of social benefits and the minimum wage, which has itself typically been linked to the average wage growth in the private sector (the "linkage law" of 1979). The "linkage" between social benefits and wages in the private sector was set aside already in 1983 and benefit levels were cut by 3 per cent and nominally frozen until 1990. As a result the gap between the average income of active and inactive people increased by more than 11 per cent between 1983 and 1988. In 1990 and 1991, the minimum wage and social benefits were again linked to wage growth in the market sector, but in 1992 a new law (WKA) made this link conditional: the Government is no longer obliged to respect the full linkage if there is "excessive" wage growth or if the number of social security beneficiaries increases to the extent that a significant hike in the rates of taxes and social security contributions is needed. For practical purposes, the law refers to the ratio of full-time equivalent beneficiaries to full-time employed persons (dependency ratio). If the dependency ratio exceeds a reference level – currently 0.83 – the Government need not respect full linkage. Hence, in 1992, with the dependency ratio expected to exceed this level, the Government was able to apply a less than full "linkage" and increase social benefits by less than private wages. In 1993 and 1994, as noted, social benefits were frozen in nominal terms, along with the minimum wage. This further increased the gap between the average income of active and inactive people. Nonetheless, incentives to find a job remain insufficient, especially at the lower end of the labour market.

The authorities have repeatedly tried to tighten the disability scheme, which is unique because of the low thresholds for entitlement, the lack of distinction between "social risk" and "professional risk",[59] and its generosity in terms of level and duration of benefits – these can continue until the age of 65, after which disabled persons move into the pension system. The rate of benefits was cut in 1984 (from 80 to 70 per cent of the last earned wage) and nominal benefits were frozen from 1984 to 1990, along with other changes in the scheme. In 1991, the Government announced a major package of measures altering various aspects of the system of social protection and, more specifically, addressing the question of disability, which was widely perceived as getting out of hand and becoming unsustainable. The package included: financial incentives to discourage the use of the sick leave and disability schemes by both employers and employees (''bonus-malus system''); a reduction in the generosity of the disability system (with benefits at the level of 70 per cent of last annual earnings limited to a fixed number of years, and then declining to only 70 per cent of the legal minimum wage plus an additional age-related allowance); and a more stringent control of sick leave and access to the disability scheme (redefinition of ''disability''), combined with the obligation for beneficiaries who are already in the scheme to be re-examined on the basis of these more stringent rules, and the obligation for those who are only partly disabled to accept all ''normal'' jobs. Part of the package was implemented in March 1992 but the remainder – *i.e.* the bills concerning the sickness scheme (TZ) and the level of benefits in the disability scheme (TBA) – was approved by Parliament, in a modified form, only in early 1993 and implemented in the second half of that year. The main difference between the approved version of the disability bill and the original version was that the level of benefits for people already in the scheme was not reduced, while for new claimants the reduction in benefit levels was made more severe. The period during which new claimants will receive a full benefit was substantially shortened; and the relationship between the replacement ratio and the number of years the claimant has worked was made less generous.[60]

The authorities do not expect the modification of the original proposal concerning the disability scheme to have a major influence on achieving the goal of reactivating persons already in the scheme. They regard the new definition of ''disability'' and the extended obligation for beneficiaries to accept all ''normal'' jobs as being far more important. Similarly, the fact that the social partners have largely ''repaired'' – *i.e.* reintroduced through collective agreements – the reduc- tion in the level of disability benefits is not regarded by the authorities as having a large impact. They stress that the cost of disability is now part of the bargaining process and much more perceptible at the company level. Therefore, there will be an incentive to reduce the number of disabled persons. Since the last part of the reform of the disability and sickness schemes went into effect only in August 1993 (for the disability scheme) and in 1994 (for the sickness scheme), it is too early to assess the impact of these changes on the number of disabled and to know whether they have caused a diversion of beneficiaries to other social security programmes – such as the normal unemployment scheme, which does not require people above $57\frac{1}{2}$ years of age to seek a job. The original aim of the reform was to limit the number of disabled to 977 000 (or 825 000 in full-time equivalents, representing over 10 per cent of the labour force) in 1994, with an expected combined saving from the disability and sick leave schemes of some Gld 4 billion in 1994. However, the number of disabled did not grow as much as expected in 1992-93 – perhaps a reaction to the announced tightening of the scheme – and, despite the delayed implementation of the reform, the authorities revised downward their projections for 1994, first to 821 000 full-time equivalents and, more recently, to 810 000 full-time equivalents. Owing to the delayed implementation, the expected saving has been reduced to Gld 2¼ billion in 1994. For the coming years, the authorities expect only a very modest decline in the number of disabled. To go beyond that and achieve a major and sustained decrease would seem to require new, more ambitious legislation or a much stricter application of existing rules.

The already considerable influence of the social partners in the implementation of Dutch labour-market policy has been further increased by recent changes in the institutional setting. In 1990 the Public Employment Service (PES) was reorganised into a body institutionally independent from the government, fully tripartite, decentralised, and no longer holding a placement monopoly. The authorities hope that this approach will improve the effectiveness of job finding, and reduce mismatches in local labour markets. It is also hoped that the employers and unions will share the responsibilities of tackling unemployment and other labour-market problems by effective placement and training measures. However, the imposition of sanctions when benefit claimants fail to accept jobs or retraining, remains the responsibility of the Industrial Insurance Boards and municipalities (GSD); the PES is obliged to notify these two bodies when such failures occur, but in practice it does not always do so.

In addition to sharing power with the government in many tripartite institutions – like the PES – the social partners directly manage and control some major institutions, such as the Industrial Insurance Boards. The ''social partnership'' creates checks and balances, emphasises consensus and the national interest, and seeks to foster social cohesion. However, the complexity of decision-making procedures creates risks for the effectiveness of labour-market policy and management. For instance, while central government legislation describes the terms and conditions under which unemployment, sickness, and disability benefits are to be granted, the Industrial Insurance Boards, over which the central government has limited control, are in charge of the actual administration. Hence, the intention of legislation can be undermined at the implementation stage, and when the interests of the individual workers and firms diverge from the public interest, it can result in unintended uses of the system, as apparently has been the case in the granting of disability benefits. A similar situation prevails in respect of the implementation of active employment policies.[61] In sum, while better cooperation between all the institutions concerned is needed and would indeed represent a distinct improvement, it is doubtful whether a major tightening of the social security system can be achieved without reducing the degree of control the social partners have on implementation.

The task ahead

The above discussion shows that although the authorities have taken many initiatives in recent years, major rigidities of an institutional, legal and contractual nature still stifle the labour market and the Dutch economy in general. With respect to the labour market and particularly its lower-end, impediments and problems can be grouped under three headings: first, restricted competition – including stringent job protection legislation – and excessive spending on welfare which result in high wage and non-wage labour costs; second, weak incentives to seek a job owing to high net social security benefits compared with take-home pay; and third, a lack of appropriate skills and qualifications, pointing to problems with the educational system – broadly defined to include apprenticeships and vocational training – and to insufficient ''active'' labour market policies. The level of unemployment, especially in its broad definition, is disturbing, and although its recent sharp rise is largely due to the economic downturn, past experience has shown that without sufficient flexibility cyclical unemployment tends to become structural. Moreover, the inflow of immigrants increases the number of unskilled persons, and globalisation – although not yet fully understood – also lends a sense of urgency to the problem.

The Dutch authorities are fully aware of the need of adapting in a rapidly changing and integrated world. Indeed, they are determined to accelerate greatly their efforts to make the whole economy more competitive, flexible and dynamic. Macroeconomic policy, of which wage moderation is seen as a key element, is designed to provide overall conditions conducive to employment growth. Stepped up investment in the infrastructure and more support for R&D should promote better conditions for job creation. Unemployment policy as such is largely targeted to specific labour-market groups with a poor prospect of finding a job. Moreover, there is a perception that full employment can only be regained if in addition to high-quality, knowledge-intensive employment low-productivity jobs in the sheltered sector of the economy are also created. Hence, in addition to deregulating the labour market and product markets, the "activating" content of the social security system must be boosted, through more "active" labour-market programmes, less "passive" income-support measures, and better financial incentives to find a job. To achieve these goals, an impressive array of initiatives are being proposed or considered.

In the view of the authorities, abolishing the automatic legal extension of sectoral wage agreements would be a major step in the direction of a better working labour market (Annex I). This move, by increasing competition, would contribute to reducing the existing gap between the legal minimum wage and the minimum wage in collective agreements. The Government has recently sent to Parliament a discussion paper proposing, for the next cabinet period, not to extend the wage component of sectoral collective agreements, and limit the extension to so-called "good causes" – *i.e.* schooling and training, provisions aimed at improving employment in general or of specific groups such as ethnic minorities and disabled persons. To liberalise hiring legislation, the Government has decided to replace the requirement of prior approval of dismissal with the right of workers to appeal dismissals in court. Also, the Government has asked advice of the Social Economic Council and the Central Board of the Public Employment Service on abolishing the license system for temporary work agencies and private counselling agencies. To improve labour mobility, a bill has been submitted to Parliament prescribing that when changing jobs the value of accumulated pension rights has to be estimated and can be transferred to the new employer who has to accept this value in terms of his own pension system. On part-time work, the Government agrees with the view of the social partners that it can meet the growing need of both employers and employees for more flexibility, and hence it is to be encouraged at the decentralised level and on a voluntary, rather than on a statutory basis. The current freeze of the legal minimum wage, although not a form of liberalisation, will nonetheless contribute to the reduction of labour costs for low-skilled workers, thereby increasing wage differentiation.

Incentives to work are still insufficient and should be strengthened by widening the net income difference between wages and social benefits. This could be done in various ways, including tax deductions for work expenses[62] and a less than full "linkage" between social benefits and wages. Also, efforts need to be stepped up to ensure that access to social security schemes is restricted to those who can prove that they are entitled to a benefit. The Government has agreed with the Buurmeijer Commission that the implementation of social security laws should be monitored by a board fully independent of the social partners and the institutions they control. The law regulating the implementation of social security schemes (OSV) is now being revised and should become effective in its new form in 1995. Among other changes it will include the obligation for the Industrial Boards and the Public Employment Service to cooperate, and will require administering bodies to reduce benefits whenever recipients do not meet the obligation of applying for work or are not fully cooperative. Over the longer term, it is envisaged to replace the Industrial Boards with regional administering bodies which would operate in "close harmony" with the Public Employment Services (which also operates on a regional basis). This administrative set-up would ensure a "one-counter approach", combining the granting of benefits with schooling, training and job-searching services.

With respect to skills and qualifications, the authorities are putting more emphasis on apprenticeships, on-the-job training and the schooling of low qualified persons. More specifically, the Government and the social partners have recently agreed on a three-year action programme to increase the number of apprentices. A new policy has been proposed calling on schools, municipalities and employment offices for additional efforts to guide school leavers back to school or to a job. Labour-market programmes, such as the "Labour pools" are being reoriented to achieve an increased through-flow of long-term unemployed. These efforts to increase labour force skills and competencies are complemented by measures, such as temporary wage cost subsidies, aimed at the creation of low-skilled jobs for the unemployed. However, such subsidies have been available for some time and they have been used only to a limited extent. Employers may see recruitment as a long-term commitment for which temporary cost reductions are not sufficiently attractive; and for the unemployed, to be attractive, these jobs must carry the prospect of more lasting employment.

IV. Conclusions

The economy is emerging from a downturn which has been shallow, both compared with previous ones and with developments in surrounding countries. This has largely reflected the pattern of specialisation of the Dutch economy, marked by a comparatively important share of industrial food production and services which are less sensitive to cyclical variations. The weak economic growth recorded in 1993 was entirely accounted for by an improvement in the foreign balance which outweighed a decline in total domestic demand. Exports were underpinned both by their product-mix and the competitive pricing policy of Dutch firms which, confronted with a strong guilder, accepted a reduction in profit margins. Business investment was especially weak but private consumption was more resilient than in most other European countries, and the savings ratio dropped to an unusually low level. Cost-price performance improved appreciably reflecting, among other factors, slack labour market conditions, a positive impact of fiscal measures and a new central agreement between the social partners to promote wage moderation. The downturn has dealt a heavy blow to the labour market which was already suffering from major structural problems. The impact on the number of persons employed has been cushioned by a further increase in part-time work, but as the labour force has continued to grow at a brisk pace, unemployment has risen rapidly.

The outlook has distinctly improved over the past few months, but the economy seems to be heading towards only a gradual recovery. The leading indicators, and in particular investment surveys for 1994, are still weak although the degree of capacity utilisation has risen significantly in the first quarter of the year. GDP growth is projected to pick up only moderately this year before accelerating in 1995, to $2\frac{3}{4}$ per cent. The driving force of the upturn is buoyant world trade and, at a later stage, a recovery in domestic investment. Business investment should pick up following an improved sales outlook, better profit margins as a result of restructuring and wage moderation, and somewhat declining interest rates. The relaxation of fiscal policy in 1994 will also support public investment. Hence, the recovery should be broadly-based and can be expected to be accompanied by further progress towards wage moderation as agreed by the social partners. On the other hand, it may not be sufficiently strong to reduce unemployment significantly. The risks attaching to this projection seem to be about balanced.

Economic policy, on balance, may have a moderately expansionary impact on activity. Confidence in the guilder, which was already underpinned by the close exchange rate link with the Deutschemark, seems to have strengthened further as a result of the ERM crisis. Dutch interest rates are among the lowest in Europe, both in nominal and real terms. Short-term rates are projected to decline further, in line with German rates. After their recent upturn, long-term rates may also decline again but at a very slow pace. Fiscal policy is set to ease in 1994. The Netherlands has been more successful than most other European countries in pursuing fiscal consolidation in the recent difficult period: last year, despite the economic downturn and the rise in unemployment, the central government deficit fell below the 1989 Coalition Accord target. But the "collective burden" (the share of taxes and social security contributions in Net National Income) is one of the highest in the OECD area and remained well above its ceiling, also set by the Coalition Accord, holding back the economy and the labour market in particular. The Government has thus decided to rearrange its priorities: it has revised upward its deficit target for 1994; and, in addition to introducing a medium-term public investment programme to improve the infrastructure – the so-called "investment impulse" – it has announced substantial reductions in taxes and social security contributions. Hence, the OECD Secretariat is projecting, on the basis of announced policies, an increase in the general government deficit this year – to 3.9 per cent of GDP – followed by a small reduction in 1995 as the economic recovery accelerates.

The announced fiscal measures aim at promoting wage moderation, maintaining an equitable income distribution and redressing the incentive balance between working and not working. More specifically, according to the authorities, they should reduce the "collective burden", boost employment and support the recovery. While all these goals are broadly commendable, one of the requirements of the Maastricht agreement is that the public debt/GDP ratio be reduced to

60 per cent in 1996 or, at least, be set on a sufficiently downward trend. This ratio increased slightly last year – to over 80 per cent – and to set it on a sufficiently downward trend further fiscal consolidation will be needed in coming years. Moreover, as noted in last year's Survey, wage moderation, although highly desirable, cannot be a substitute for more fundamental measures to correct structural imbalances. In view of the size of problems in the labour market and the social security system, a thorough-going reform is needed, including major cuts in welfare expenditure. This would allow fiscal policy to reach its various targets and goals which under present conditions are somewhat conflicting.

In contrast with its good performance on the macroeconomic side, economic policy has been distinctly less successful in correcting structural rigidities and distortions. Although a large number of initiatives have been taken, notably in the area of disability and competition policy, on balance, progress has been slow. Moreover, the piecemeal approach adopted with respect to the interrelated problems in the labour market and welfare system seems inadequate in view of the gravity of the situation. As noted, the downturn has exacerbated long-lasting problems in the labour market which is now unquestionably the weak spot of an otherwise fundamentally healthy economy.

Labour market performance has deteriorated strongly over the past two decades since the standardised unemployment rate has risen from less than 1 per cent in 1970 to around 10 per cent currently, and many indicators suggest that unemployment has risen markedly between successive cycles – *i.e.* that most of it is of a structural nature and cannot be expected to be corrected by economic growth alone. Moreover, the effective rate of unemployment is considerably higher. For instance, including all unemployed and inactive persons of working age receiving a disability pension or other social security benefits and persons enrolled in special job creation programmes ("broad unemployment"), the rate currently exceeds 26 per cent, compared with less than 8 per cent in 1970. Standardised unemployment is characterised by a very uneven incidence, with a high share of low-skilled, female and long-term unemployment. The relative unemployment of older persons has declined but this has been due to the large inflow of older persons into early retirement programmes and disability. Disability is probably the most striking feature of the Dutch labour market. It represents the largest component of broad unemployment (over 10 percentage points, in full-time equivalents), with nearly one million persons receiving benefits, in a country of 15 million inhabitants. Another key feature of the Dutch labour market is the rising importance of part-time workers who account for 35 per cent of total employment, by far the highest in the OECD area. However, to the extent that part-time work is involuntary it is not a satisfactory solution. While the Netherlands has created many more jobs than other European countries on average, the participation rate, in full-time equivalents, has remained very low. And the non-employment rate (*i.e.* the difference between the population of working age and employment, in full-time equivalents, as a percentage of the former), has increased over time and, at nearly 50 per cent, is extremely high by international standards. The direct budgetary cost of broad unemployment represents nearly 10 per cent of GDP, with disability accounting for over 40 per cent of this figure. This may also help explain why over the last decade the rate of growth of per capita real GDP has been significantly below the EC and OECD averages.

The persistence of high structural unemployment has been the result of a variety of complex and often interacting factors which have built up over several years or decades. They can be grouped under three broad headings: high labour costs, reflecting both excessive wages – especially at the lower end of the market – and heavy social security contributions; insufficient incentives to work, owing to generous social welfare benefits and the tax system; and other rigidities and mismatches. One set of reasons why wages have not shown more flexibility in the face of persistent unemployment relate to institutional, legal and contractual features of wage-setting, *i.e.* the administrative extension of sectoral wage agreements and the minimum legal wage. These rigidities have effectively prevented the unemployed (outsiders) from bidding for lower wages. The generosity of welfare programmes – in terms of eligibility and benefits – have affected the labour market in several ways. Because of their budgetary cost, these programmes have increased social security contributions, thereby adding to labour costs. Moreover, unemployment and other welfare programmes, by reducing the financial incentive to find a job, seem to have encouraged broad unemployment and decreased downward pressure on wages, especially for low-skilled workers. Insufficient incentives to work have been aggravated by the high effective marginal tax rates implicit in income-dependent subsidies. Other rigidities include primarily employment security legislation which is rather stringent in comparison with other European countries. As for labour mismatches – broadly defined – a lack of appropriate skills and qualifications may have played an increasingly important role as a result of the acceleration of technological progress and the growing inflow of immigrants and asylum seekers.

Despite this impressive list of rigidities which hamper the labour market, in many respects the performance of the Dutch economy has remained good: a strong currency, a large current-account surplus, and improved public finances. In a way, the economy has developed a "dual" character. Confronted with excessive labour costs, enterprises have responded by substituting capital for labour, restructuring and shifting production abroad. They have succeeded in increasing productivity, restoring profit margins, and preserving international competitiveness, but the counterpart has been a destruction of jobs. The new broad "equilibrium" does not entail a satisfactory utilisation of the labour force. Wage moderation in the second half of the 1980s has favoured employment but has not been sufficient. Many workers, especially low-skilled ones, have priced themselves out of the market. Thus, the root of the problem is at the lower end of the labour market but, because of the social security contributions needed to support these unemployed persons, this sectoral imbalance leads to high labour costs in the whole economy, jeopardising employment at all levels. The tax wedge – at around 45 per cent – is strikingly higher than the European and OECD averages. At the risk of oversimplification, it can be said that, confronted like all other industrialised countries with the problem of unemployment, the Netherlands has gone further than most of them in emphasising equity and other social considerations rather than economic efficiency. Hence, a special effort has been made to insulate the labour force from the hardship of adjusting to changing market conditions. However commendable on social grounds, this approach may have become economically unsustainable.

In today's rapidly integrating world, a small very open economy like the Dutch one, has little choice but to allow market forces to operate more fully and adapt better to change. Several additional factors lend urgency to the situation: a sustained increase in the labour force in coming years, as a result of demographic forces and a large inflow of immigrants and asylum seekers over which the Netherlands has little control; the prospect of only moderate economic growth over the medium-term; and the risk that without sufficient labour-market flexibility the recent steep increase in unemployment, although largely cyclical, might become structural. Reflecting the complexity of the problem, and its long-lasting character, what is needed is a comprehensive, in depth, multi-year reform. In a nutshell, the goal should be to reduce labour costs, redress the incentive balance between working and not working, and improve labour force skills and competencies, in all cases especially at the lower end of the market.

To achieve these goals, competition in the labour market must be stepped-up, notably by abolishing the automatic legal extension of sectoral wage agreements, loosening job protection legislation, and further reducing the relevance of the legal minimum wage. Since fiscal consolidation prevents substantial cuts in taxes and social security contributions without at the same time cutting public expenditure, a better focused welfare system is the key to redressing the incentive balance and lowering non-wage labour costs. The scope and need for correction is especially important in the area of disability: while further reductions in benefit levels may be needed, priority should be given to the tightening of eligibility conditions and their enforcement, with a re-examination of people already in the scheme by an independent medical panel. The aim cannot be a mere stabilisation of the number of disabled but a sustained reduction, since their current level seems totally out of line with the general health status of the population and unjustified by any other objective criteria. The "linkage" between legal minimum wage and minimum social benefits should be loosened or phased out. As for the unemployment benefits scheme, benefits should be conditional on recipients applying for work, participating in "active" programmes and fully cooperating with the Public Employment Service. Moreover, a thorough reorganisation of the institutions in charge of administering social security laws may be necessary to avoid, as apparently has been the case in the past, the intention of legislation being undermined at the implementation stage. A second needed element is the introduction of a "one-counter system" – combining the payment of benefits, placement and counselling services, and the management of training programmes – to increase the effectiveness of "active" measures and labour-market policies in general. An additional element would be to give the social security institutions more incentive to be active in facilitating the return of claimants to the active labour market and to introduce competition between the public employment service and private agencies. With respect to skills and qualifications, more emphasis should be put on apprenticeship, on-the-job training, and the schooling of low qualified persons (the school to work transition). In addition, special efforts may be needed to tackle the problem of school drop-outs and asylum seekers. More generally, the Netherlands is currently an outlier among OECD countries in its emphasis on "passive" relative to "active" labour-market policies, and this mix needs to be decisively rebalanced towards measures which assist re-employment. This means that tightening the welfare system may not, by itself allow social security contributions to be cut substantially until the number of persons on welfare declines as a result of better incentives to work and a more flexible and competitive labour market. Hence, to the extent that the goal of fiscal consolidation allows it, it is essential to reduce taxes and social security contributions, with an emphasis on the lower end of the wage scale.

This wide-ranging reform of the labour market and welfare system, which is broadly in line with measures already proposed or envisaged by the Government, should be complemented by deregulation and increased competition in goods and services markets, including in the public sector. The implementation of competition policy has been stepped up and legislation is moving closer to that of the majority of OECD Member countries, although control of mergers and acquisitions is still not envisaged. Efforts of the authorities in this area are welcome, but aligning Dutch competition policy with the EC remains a gradual and long process, and ways should be considered to speed it up. The ongoing process of introducing market forces in the public sector should also be pursued, if not accelerated, especially in the housing market, public transport, utilities and health care. Also, steps to foster entrepreneurship and small business should be considered – for instance, to lower start-up costs, simplify compliance requirements and enhance the availability of venture capital.

Most of the required measures are mutually reinforcing. For instance, benefit cuts at the central level cannot help in reducing the tax wedge on labour if the umbrella organisations set up sectoral-level schemes – as they have done for early retirement and for the recent cuts in social security benefits. Hence, by proceeding simultaneously on a broad front it should be possible to enhance the efficacy of the measures adopted and set in motion a virtuous circle which would minimise the unavoidable cost of adjustment. This approach, by involving practically all segments of society, could offer the added advantage of creating a bond of solidarity, thereby avoiding acute problems of equity. Nonetheless, at first, standards of living may be under pressure, and many of the jobs created as a result of these measures are likely to be of a low-productivity low-pay type and to be in the sheltered sector of the economy. Over the longer-run, however, a fuller utilisation of the population of working age can be expected to have important welfare gains, and to bring about healthier and more sustainable social conditions.

In conclusion, partly as a result of sound macroeconomic policies, the downturn has been mild and economic growth is expected to accelerate again this year and next. Nonetheless, the upturn is unlikely to have a major impact on the labour market which, along with the welfare system, requires an in depth structural reform. This is not to say that the Netherlands should abandon its cherished notions of equity, fairness, and solidarity; rather, that is should better balance social equity and economic efficiency, thereby preserving the essential elements of social protection, and that efforts should be made to reach equity targets with smaller losses in employment than in the past. Also, while competition must be increased in the labour market and in the economy in general, this should not be at the cost of the Dutch "consensus approach" which minimises tensions and conflicts. These are undoubtedly difficult "rebalancing" operations, but present conditions seem to offer a window of opportunity: unemployment is widely perceived as a major problem requiring correction; the projected mild recovery of the economy may facilitate the financing of stepped-up "active" measures without holding out the false hope of a painless reduction in unemployment; and the next Government – through a new Coalition Agreement – will have the possibility of forging a new medium-term policy. The challenge to the next Government is to seize this opportunity, relying on the many strengths of the Dutch economy and society, and to move towards major reforms now, rather than only if and when it is faced with the threat of an impending crisis.

Notes and references

1. Excluding net contributions (actual and imputed) to life insurance and pension schemes.

2. This reflected investment by public companies in a power generating station and off-shore oil platforms.

3. The ratio of social-security beneficiaries (in full-time equivalents) to employed persons (also in full-time equivalents).

4. The Dutch authorities have recently changed the CPI definition which has resulted in an increase in the level of inflation. The reason for the redefinition of the CPI is to better match the cost of living and to reflect the pattern of expenditure of households rather than of only working class families. The most important changes are the exclusion of insured medical care and the inclusion of certain indirect taxes, such as sewage and garbage collection charges, registration fees on cars, dog and television licence fees, etc. Also included are certain government services.

5. The share of foreign exchange in total official reserves was also boosted by the sale of nearly one quarter of the official gold stock (see Part II).

6. At the time of writing the 1989 Coalition Accord, the 1990 collective burden was expected to be 53.7 per cent of NNI, but the actual figure came out more than a full percentage point lower (52.6 per cent). Nonetheless, the expected figure for 1990 has been retained as the ceiling. The Study Group on Budget margin has recently recommended a couple of changes in the definition of the collective burden, of which the exclusion of the non-tax gas revenues is the most important. It is up to the new Government which will take office after the elections of May 1994, to decide whether or not to introduce the new definition.

7. The number of new disability claimants in the market sector declined by 9 000 in 1992 to 76 000 but rose again in 1993 to 84 000, almost the same number as before the reform (85 000 in 1991).

8. In 1992, as part of a large health care reform, insurance for pharmaceuticals was shifted from the national health care insurance scheme (for people with a wage under the "modal" wage – *i.e.* the average production worker's wage –, financed by employers and employee contributions) and from private health care insurance (for people with wages above the "modal" wage) to the national social welfare scheme called the "AWBZ". Contributions to the scheme consist of two parts: 7.5 per cent of taxable income in the first tax bracket and a lump sum premium amounting to Gld 133 per year per person.

9. Without this "cash-management" measure between 1993 and 1994, the central government deficit would have come out a full percentage point lower at 2.8 per cent of NNI. Social security is accounted on a transaction basis and does not appear on the central government accounts. The insurance funds mentioned in the text are: the General Child Allowance Fund; the General Windows and Orphans Fund; and the General Disability Fund.

10. The current Government has started to prepare the 1995 Budget which will be finalised and presented to Parliament by the new Government which will take office after the elections of May 1994.

11. The first tranche of the flotation of KNP (representing about one-third of the value of the company) took place in June 1994. It was the biggest flotation in Dutch history and raised over Gld 7 billion. The second tranche of the flotation is expected in two or three years. The aim of the Government is to reduce its shareholding to about one-third.

12. Over the medium-term, the non-recurrent factors will be replaced by structural expenditure reductions.

13. The tax lowering package for 1994 comprises a reduction in employers' contributions of Gld 2 billion (on a full-year basis), a tax reduction for small enterprises, a reduction of the first tax bracket and other improvements in the tax structure. For 1995, the Government aims at supporting wage moderation by making a further reduction in the first tax bracket (by $3/4$ percentage points at a cost of Gld 2 billion), dependent on wage growth being moderate in 1994 and 1995.

14. The cost of the sickness scheme has been transferred from the government account to the employers; enterprises are legally obliged to continue to pay wages for the first six weeks in case of sickness leave.

15. Only investment in roads and waterways will be statistically recorded as public investment. Investment in the infrastructure for railways and other public transports – such as subways and bus lanes – will be recorded as business investment.

16. The Dutch Government has a claim on the German *"Brigitta Erdgas und Erdöhl"* due to its excess use of the common (border) natural gas source.

17. Both in 1986-90 and 1990-94, according to OECD Secretariat calculations, the Netherlands comes close to the 45 degree line, indicating that automatic stabilisers are being offset by discretionary fiscal measures.

18. These two years connect peaks in the unemployment rate.

19. In February 1993, against the background of pressure on the budget from interest payments and in the light of requirements imposed on national fiscal policy by the Maastricht Treaty, the Minister of Finance asked the Study Group on the Budget margin for advice on the need to control the budget deficit and the level of government debt.

20. The Dutch experience with the structural fiscal policy pursued in the 1970s was mixed, as it did not prevent an escalation in the budget deficit, mainly due to over optimistic medium-term revenue projections. Hence, the Study Group strongly advises the use of a "cautious" scenario of medium-term economic developments.

21. These comparative price levels are defined as the ratios of PPPs to exchange rates.

22. See Chapter III, OECD (1991/1992), *Economic Survey, Netherlands.*

23. Standardised unemployment.

24. In full-time equivalents.

25. This is true when unemployment is defined in a "broad" rather than in a "narrow" sense, for many older people have moved into special welfare programmes and withdrawn from the labour force.

26. These withdrawals, in full-time equivalents, have increased from some 200 000, or a little over 4 per cent of the labour force, in 1970 to nearly 1 million, or over 17 per cent of the labour force, in 1992.

27. The share of employment in manufacturing has declined from 26 per cent in 1975 to 18 per cent in 1992.

28. If part-time unemployment is defined – as it is done in the Netherlands – as employees working more than 12 hours but less than 35 hours per week, its share in total employment is somewhat lower (less than 25 per cent in 1992).

29. In 1990, 89 per cent of employees were covered by agreements on the reduction of normal working hours.

30. *Delors Report*, page 149. According to another measurement, for dependent employment in the Netherlands the average hours actually worked per person per year declined by 11 per cent from 1979 to 1991, while the average of France, Germany, Spain and the United States declined by 6.8 per cent. Hence, average hours per person in the Netherlands which represented 89 per cent of the average of the above countries in 1979, represented only 85 per cent in 1991 (Table B, OECD [1993], *Employment Outlook*).

31. For full-time workers, however, the difference is marginal: an average of 39 hours of work a week in the Netherlands compared with 40 hours in Europe on average.

32. Table 1.6, OECD (1993), *Employment Outlook*.

33. That is, recording partly disabled persons in full-time equivalents.

34. Table 1.5, OECD (1993), *Employment Outlook*.

35. In Belgium, the budgetary cost of broad unemployment, defined in a similar way, represents $3^1/_2$ per cent of GDP. As for the cost of disability, according to Eurostat, it represented 6 per cent of GDP in the Netherlands and 2.7 per cent in EC countries on average. But, contrary to most other countries, in the Netherlands welfare benefits are subject to taxes.

36. Another important reason, however, may have been the relatively low degree of competition. This was the structural topic of the 1993 Survey.

37. Excluding mining, quarrying and the gas sector.

38. Table 13, OECD (1993), *The Labour Market in the Netherlands*.

39. In the Netherlands, there is also relatively little wage differentiation between sectors.

40. It is the social charges which account for the high tax wedge in the Netherlands. But the composition of the tax wedge cannot be compared internationally since countries have a different fiscalisation of social security costs.

41. OECD (1994), *The OECD Jobs Study*.

42. More generally, the Dutch authorities view globalisation as a major force acting in today's world. Hence, in March 1994, they organised a conference on this topic – the so-called Platform Globalisation – bringing together representatives of employers, unions, private experts and politicians. The conference stressed the need for both firms and government to step up their efforts to better use the pool of talent available in the country and make the Dutch economy more competitive.

43. According to press reports, this seems to have been the case in the recent decision of Mercedes-Benz to locate its new plant in Germany rather than abroad.

44. Excluding Japan.

45. Graafland J.J., "Insiders and outsiders in wage formation: the Dutch case", *Empirical Economics*, volume 17, 1992.

46. See Table 3.5 in OECD (1993), *Employment Outlook*.

47. The positive effect of this measure on employment has been estimated by the Central Planning Bureau at 35 000 persons by 1990.

48. Looking at 19 OECD countries, including the Netherlands, the OECD Secretariat has found a statistical relationship between the maximum duration of unemployment benefits and long-term unemployment (Chapter III, OECD [1993], *Employment Outlook*).

49. If unemployment benefit replacement rates are calculated as the ratio of actual payments of unemployment insurance benefits to the total number of unemployed, with respect to the average wage of production workers, they have decreased from 93 per cent in 1980 to 75 per cent – still the highest level in the OECD (Table 3.1, OECD [1993], *Employment Outlook*, 1993).

50. This was the conclusion of the Dutch authorities in a recent survey of effective marginal tax rates.

51. This parliamentary commission is usually referred to as the "Buurmeijer Commission", after the name of its chairman.

52. Chapter III, OECD (1993), *Economic Survey, Netherlands*.

53. OECD (1993), *The labour market in the Netherlands*, page 15.

54. If short assignments are included in "hiring".

55. Chapter III, OECD (1993), *Employment Outlook*.

56. OECD (1991), *Employment Outlook*.

57. These are bipartite institutions (*i.e.* comprising employer and union representatives) which manage unemployment insurance schemes, sickness, insurance, and disability benefits as well as some associated "active" measures.

58. Statistical work shows an inverse correlation between the ratio of expenditures for active programmes to unemployment benefits and long-term unemployment (Chapter III, OECD [1993], *Employment Outlook*).

59. "Professional risk" concerns disability caused by industrial or occupational accidents or diseases. "Social risk" concerns disability from other causes.

60. For example, a person of 40 years of age with an income 1½ times the average will receive 40 per cent less than under the present system – *i.e.* 50 per cent instead of 70 per cent of the previous earned income, plus an additional age-related allowance.

61. For instance, 19 Industrial Insurance Boards, some 650 municipalities and the PES (itself decentralised) all, in principle, play a role in reintegrating the unemployed into the active labour force.

62. A special Commission recently advised the use of this instrument to reduce the replacement rate and generate employment of low-skilled workers.

Annex I

The unemployment problem: policy simulations

To analyze the unemployment problem and in particular the interaction between the tax system, the social security system, and the labour market, the Central Planning Bureau (CPB) has built an integrated micro- and macro-general equilibrium model with strong emphasis on the institutional context (MIMIC, *i.e.* MIcro Macro model to analyze the Institutional Context). This model is based on the theory of imperfect labour markets and distinguishes 16 types of households and six sectors – of which the exposed and the sheltered sectors are the most important ones. Labour supply and labour demand are described as search strategies of the unemployed and firms, respectively. Demand and supply for the five types of labour come together in the matching function.[1] The search strategy of the unemployed consists of two parts: search intensity and reservation wage. As the unemployed attach positive value to leisure and income, their search intensity rises with a fall in unemployment benefits. Furthermore, a fall in unemployment benefits reduces the reservation wage and hence the unemployed are more willing to accept a job. Both the increase in search intensity and lower reservation wage diminish search costs for employers, thus strengthening their bargaining power in collective wage negotiations. In the search strategy of firms at the lower end of the labour market, the effective minimum wage plays a key role. It defines the number of jobs created by the employer by imposing a minimum level of labour productivity which is required to meet the minimum wage. The employer accepts more low skilled workers if the effective minimum wage falls. The search cost of acceptable workers decreases with a fall in relative minimum benefits, improving the bargaining power of employers in the collective wage negotiations. Crucial features in the model are the labour supply elasticities between groups: breadwinners and singles have an inelastic labour supply, while that for partners – usually women – is very high, but inversely related to the net income of the breadwinner (see Table). The collective wage bargaining system between unions and employers' organisations similar to the "right-to-manage model" of Nickell and Andrews (1983) exists. In addition to employers' search costs, important factors determining wages are the ratio between consumer and producer prices, the unemployment rate, the net replacement rate, and the average and marginal tax rates. A higher unemployment rate and a lower replacement rate weaken the bargaining position of the unions and affect wages negatively. A higher average tax rate increases the wage claims of unions in order to offset the fall in purchasing power. In contrast to an increase in the average tax rate, an increase in the marginal rate has a negative effect on wage outcomes. This shows the presence of the

113

theory of second best in the model: in an imperfect market model, one distortion (marginal tax rates) can relieve another (collective wage formation). In the trade-off between net income and employment, a higher marginal tax rate favours the latter and makes unions more willing to accept lower wages in exchange for higher employment.

Some crucial elasticities in the labour market of MIMIC

	Elasticity
Elasticities of labour supply with respect to:	
Wage of breadwinners	0.0
Wage of partners	1.00
Other-income (family income) of partners	−0.30
Elasticities of wages with respect to:	
Consumer prices	0.50
Average rate of taxes and premiums	0.50
Marginal rate of taxes	−0.06
Unemployment rate	−1.00
Net replacement	0.25

The model can be used to simulate the labour-market effects of various policy actions to reduce unemployment: for example, a decrease in the minimum wage; tax reductions through lowering tax rates and through an increase in the general labour cost deduction; and a drastic overhaul of the social security scheme, resulting in a so-called "mini-system" or safety net system. In all scenarios, offsetting fiscal measures are assumed in order to obtain budget neutral effects.

A lowering of the legal minimum wage alone[2] has only modest effects. A 10 per cent cut in the legal minimum wages reduces the lowest sectoral wage scales by only 2.5 per cent. If the sectoral minimum wage scales were to fall in line with the legal minimum wage – for example, as a result of abolishing the automatic extension of sectoral wage contracts – the effects would be three to four times greater. Nevertheless, the effects remain limited, as the reservation wage and replacement rates are not affected, and hence search activity and the effective labour supply are not increased.

A lowering of the tax rate in the first bracket is more effective in reducing unemployment than lowering rates in higher tax brackets, as the unemployment problem is concentrated at the lower end of the labour market and a more progressive tax system induces wage moderation. As a result of lower wage increases, more employment is created. However, the net impact on unemployment remains relatively limited because the labour supply of women increases and because a tax reduction does not affect the replacement rate. In this respect, a tax reduction through an increase in the general worker's deduction is more effective, as it decreases the replacement ratio and it lowers the reservation wage and thus moderates wages more strongly. Overall labour productivity declines, reflecting substitution of low-skilled labour for high-skilled labour. However, the efficacy of this instrument is limited, as the effects of further deductions become progressively smaller.

A major overhaul of the current welfare system, resulting in a safety net system, including a negative income tax would solve the unemployment problem. In addition, a negative income tax system would have some advantages over the current system, such as transparency, a total individualisation of benefit schemes with equal treatment of men and women, and no problems with entitlement rules, abuse and fraud. In the scenario calculated by the CPB, the negative income tax is set at 50 per cent of the current minimum wage for everyone above 18 years of age. Last-wage-related government social security schemes are abolished, although it is assumed that unions reinsure the risk of disability for 50 per cent and that for unemployment for only 10 per cent.[3] The counter-argument most commonly put forward against such a system is its cost, necessitating high increases in taxes. According to the MIMIC, these effects would remain limited or even reversed, as they depend crucially on the negative income tax level. With a level of 50 per cent of the current minimum wage, the number of beneficiaries would decrease by almost 10 per cent and the rate of the flat income tax would have to be 51 per cent, representing a reduction of almost 10 percentage points compared with the current average level. The unemployment problem would disappear as a result of a fall in labour supply – the basic income dissuading many partners from entering the labour market – and an increase in employment. The increase in employment would reflect a wider wage differentiation, improving the allocation function of wages in matching demand and supply of labour.

In conclusion, according to the CPB model, the introduction of a negative income tax is very effective as it hits the Dutch system precisely in its weak point – the generosity and lenient entitlement rules of the welfare state which distorts the working of the labour market, in particular for low-skilled workers. However, a negative income tax would imply large income redistribution effects: the current unemployed and disabled would suffer a major cut in their incomes, while current inactive people without a benefit (*i.e.* most housewives) would gain.

Notes

1. The matching function describes the number of vacancies filled from contacts between employers offering a job and unemployed workers seeking a job.
2. This means that the social security benefits are not proportionately reduced.
3. This assumption reflects the reaction of the unions to the 1987 reform of the unemployment insurance schemes which was significantly weaker than the reaction to the 1993 disability reform.

Annex II

Calendar of main economic events

1993

January

Legal opening hours for shops are extended from 6:00 p.m. to 6:30 pm.

Excise taxes on diesel are increased by Gld 0.11 a litre.

In order to comply with EC directives to harmonise VAT rates between EC member states, the Government re-orders the categories of goods covered by lower and standard rates.

The special indirect tax on cars, additional to the VAT-tax, is replaced by a registration fee (BPM) to prevent tax evasion through cross-border shopping in other EC countries after elimination of the internal borders. The BPM rate on cars is 45.2 per cent of the car's catalogue value, minus Gld 3394 and Gld 1278 for petrol and diesel respectively.

The Government introduces an "Industry Facility" to increase the supply of high-risk capital for high-tech business projects. The Government contributes Gld 200 million, and financial companies another Gld 680 million. The loans, restricted to Gld 50 million per enterprise, will be offered at market interest rates.

The usual half year's increase in social security benefits linked to the private wage growth does not take place.

February

The central bank converts 400 tonnes of gold reserves, nearly a quarter of its total stock, into foreign exchange. The proceeds of the operation amount to $4.3 billion.

The Ministry of Finance announces that, in compliance with EC legislation, all financial institutions will be subject to a new law aimed at preventing money laundering. It requires financial institutions to provide information on suspicious transactions of over Gld 250 000.

The Dutch truck manufacturer DAF goes bankrupt. A new company "DAF trucks" is created out of DAF which continues the still profitable production of heavy goods vehicles.

April

The German DASA, the aircraft subsidiary of Mercedes Benz, attains a majority stake in the aircraft manufacturer Fokker.

July

Horizontal price agreements are prohibited by a general decree under the existing Economic Competition Act of 1956 (see Part II).

The usual half year's increase in social security benefits linked to the private wage growth does not take place.

August

ERM currency fluctuation margins are widened to 15 per cent of central rates, but in a bilateral agreement between the Netherlands and Germany, it is decided that the guilder-Deutschemark fluctuation margins remain unchanged at $2^{1}/4$ per cent (see Part II).

The last part of the disability scheme reform concerning the level of the benefits is implemented (see Part III).

September

The 1994 Budget is presented to Parliament. It aims at achieving the upward revised budget target deficit of $3^{3}/4$ per cent of Net National Income in 1994; and includes budget savings amounting to 12 billion (See Part II).

November

The Government eases investment rules for the General Government Pension Fund (ABP), allowing it to invest up to 10 per cent of its funds abroad.

The social partners agree on a central wage agreement stating that there will be little or no room for nominal wage increases in 1994 (see Part I).

1994

January

The central bank decides that it will no longer accept paper for discounting and, therefore, the discount rate ceases to exist. The discount rate on promissory notes will be maintained as a reference rate for legal purposes in defining lending rates, and will be set equal to the interest rate on advances plus 0.5 percentage point.

As part of a disability and sickness reform, enterprises are legally obliged, in case of sickness, to pay the first six weeks of benefits (which are no longer insured by the sickness scheme). The usual half year's increase in social security benefits linked to the private wage growth does not take place.

The Government decides to refuse 12 requests for an exception on the general ban on horizontal price agreements.

February

In the Spring budgetary note, the Ministry of Finance confirms a tax windfall amounting to Gld 5.2 billion in 1993. Hence, the Government decides to return the permanent (or structural) part of the windfall to the tax payer by lowering the employers' social security contributions by 1.4 percentage points and the employees' contributions by 0.25 percentage point. Furthermore, corporate tax rates for small corporations are brought more in line with those for larger corporations by shortening the first tax bracket with a higher rate (40 per cent), from Gld 250 000 to Gld 100 000.

To ensure a more permanent "sterilisation" of the excess liquidity created by official intervention in the foreign exchange market in the summer of 1993, the central bank starts issuing interest-bearing negotiable bank certificates.

April

The Government announces additional budget savings for 1995 amounting to Gld 1.7 billion, which partly offset the higher than foreseen cost for receiving asylum seekers and lower than expected gas export revenues.

May

National elections are held. The current Coalition Government of Christian Democrats and Social Democrats loses its majority in Parliament. Although losing 12 seats, the Social Democrats (PvdA) become the largest party with 37 seats. The Christian Democrats (CDA) lose 20 seats and become the second largest party with 34 seats. The Liberals (VVD) and D'66, with 31 seats and 24 seats, respectively, gain 9 seats and 12 seats.

STATISTICAL AND STRUCTURAL ANNEX

Selected background statistics

	Average 1985-93	1985	1986	1987	1988	1989	1990	1991	1992	1993
A. Per cent changes from previous year										
Private consumption[1]	2.5	2.4	2.6	2.7	0.8	3.5	4.2	3.0	2.1	0.8
Gross fixed capital formation[1]	2.7	6.7	6.9	0.9	4.5	4.9	1.6	0.4	1.1	-2.8
Public[1]	0.8	-3.6	-7.2	2.2	5.2	0.5	6.7	-0.8	4.9	-1.1
Residential[1]	1.2	-0.4	3.7	1.9	11.3	0.7	-2.5	-8.8	4.3	0.8
Business[1]	4.0	13.2	11.6	0.2	1.6	7.8	2.4	4.4	-0.8	-4.4
GDP[1]	2.4	2.6	2.7	1.2	2.6	4.7	4.1	2.1	1.4	0.2
Implicit price deflator:										
GDP	1.5	1.8	0.2	-0.5	1.2	1.2	2.3	2.8	2.5	1.6
Private consumption	1.7	2.2	0.3	0.2	0.5	1.2	2.2	3.4	3.0	2.1
Exports of goods and services	-2.1	1.5	-15.7	-4.7	0.5	4.5	-0.8	-0.2	-2.4	-2.0
Imports of goods and services	-2.2	1.2	-16.7	-3.0	-0.5	4.8	-1.3	0.1	-1.9	-2.2
Industrial production	2.1	4.5	2.8	0.6	5.1	4.0	3.9	-0.9	0.2	-1.5
Employment	2.1	1.3	2.5	1.6	2.9	2.0	3.3	2.6	2.0	0.8
Compensation of employees	4.1	3.2	4.4	3.4	2.7	2.9	5.9	6.1	5.5	2.6
Productivity (GDP[1]/employment)	0.9	1.0	0.7	-0.5	1.0	2.7	1.7	0.6	0.6	0.4
Unit labour costs (comp. of employees/GDP[1])	1.6	0.6	1.7	2.2	0.1	-1.7	1.7	3.9	4.1	2.4
B. Percentage ratios										
Gross fixed capital formation as % of GDP at constant prices	20.8	20.2	21.0	21.0	21.4	21.4	20.9	20.6	20.5	19.9
Stockbuilding as % of GDP at constant prices	0.5	0.7	0.8	-0.0	0.0	1.1	1.3	0.6	0.3	-0.0
Foreign balance as % of GDP at constant prices	4.4	4.1	3.4	3.2	4.0	4.0	4.6	5.2	5.2	5.8
Compensation of employees as % of GDP at current prices	52.9	52.1	52.9	54.3	53.7	52.2	51.9	52.4	53.2	53.6
Direct taxes as % of household income	12.0	10.3	10.8	10.8	11.4	11.3	12.7	14.0	13.1	13.7
Social security contributions as % of household income	19.9	21.8	20.8	21.2	21.3	19.9	17.8	18.6	19.0	19.1
Household saving as % of disposable income	2.1	-0.2	1.4	1.4	1.8	4.0	5.9	1.1	2.4	1.6
Unemployment as % of civilian labour force	8.5	10.5	9.8	9.5	9.1	8.3	7.5	7.0	6.7	8.1
C. Other indicator										
Current balance (billion dollars)	6.5	5.1	4.9	2.9	5.0	8.0	10.1	7.6	6.8	8.6

1. At constant 1990 prices.
Source: OECD Secretariat.

Table A. National product and expenditure

	1985	1986	1987	1988	1989	1990	1991	1992	1993
	Gld. million, current prices								
Private final consumption expenditure	252 914	260 240	267 931	271 633	284 470	303 075	322 986	339 511	349 414
Government final consumption expenditure	66 884	67 728	69 784	70 200	71 764	74 795	77 945	81 502	83 066
Gross fixed capital formation	83 689	89 346	91 542	97 382	104 074	107 945	110 821	114 977	112 684
Private	71 586	78 153	80 055	85 173	91 541	94 247	96 885	99 960	97 662
Government	12 103	11 193	11 487	12 209	12 533	13 698	13 936	15 017	15 022
Increase in stocks	3 097	3 993	-308	324	5 283	6 529	3 452	2 005	-730
National expenditure	406 583	421 307	428 949	439 540	465 591	492 344	515 204	537 995	544 435
Exports of goods and services	258 732	222 010	219 250	240 170	267 670	279 727	294 449	294 417	289 567
less: Imports of goods and services	238 323	205 542	207 644	222 345	248 760	255 830	267 788	269 283	261 094
Gross domestic product at market prices	425 346	437 698	440 555	457 389	484 646	516 241	541 864	563 218	573 365
less: Net indirect taxes	36 430	39 510	39 430	41 710	43 630	47 990	49 820	56 010	..
Net income from the rest of the world	-40	-680	-1 150	-3 500	-200	-910	-1 170	-1 370	..
Gross national product at factor cost	388 876	397 508	399 975	412 179	440 816	467 341	490 874	505 838	..
less: Depreciation and other operating provisions	45 977	46 982	48 786	51 453	55 153	58 528	61 834	62 094	62 194
Net national income at factor cost	342 670	350 270	351 460	361 010	385 960	409 140	429 290	440 520	..
	Gld. million, 1990 constant prices								
Private final consumption expenditure	264 381	271 248	278 669	281 018	290 820	303 097	312 274	318 792	321 342
Government final consumption expenditure	67 288	69 680	71 487	72 494	73 601	74 794	75 749	76 746	76 439
Gross fixed capital formation	89 807	95 991	96 854	101 230	106 224	107 940	108 418	109 587	106 573
Private	77 002	84 111	84 713	88 459	93 390	94 242	94 829	95 332	92 475
Government	12 805	11 880	12 141	12 771	12 834	13 698	13 589	14 255	14 098
Increase in stocks	3 134	3 865	-198	54	5 293	6 517	3 220	1 517	-100
National expenditure	424 610	440 784	446 812	454 796	475 938	492 348	499 661	506 642	504 255
Exports of goods and services	216 595	220 550	228 494	249 012	265 569	279 745	295 034	302 245	303 333
less: Imports of goods and services	198 196	205 216	213 760	230 014	245 516	255 828	267 571	274 398	272 038
Gross domestic product at market prices	444 046	456 255	461 653	473 716	495 893	516 266	527 122	534 510	535 570
less: Net indirect taxes	39 867	43 360	41 030	43 118	46 118	47 990	48 530	50 138	..
Net income from the rest of the world	-2 187	599	-4 089	-4 109	-1 342	-910	-1 865	-3 745	..
Gross national product at factor cost	401 992	413 495	416 534	426 489	448 433	467 366	476 728	480 627	..

Sources: CBS, *1992 National Accounts* and OECD Secretariat.

Table B. **Origin of net domestic product at factor cost**

Gld. million, current prices

	1985	1986	1987	1988	1989	1990	1991	1992	1993 [1]
Agriculture, forestry and fishing	13 831	15 113	14 212	14 580	17 019	17 032	17 315	16 430	15 367
Mining and quarrying (incl. nat. gas)	33 840	21 683	13 940	10 892	11 586	13 506	16 107	13 882	13 332
Manufacturing	61 857	66 497	67 623	73 186	76 798	80 398	81 226	80 793	78 749
Construction	18 255	19 623	20 390	23 277	24 416	25 538	26 223	28 388	29 277
Electricity, gas and water (excl. nat. gas)	4 407	4 578	4 807	4 785	4 716	5 088	5 425	5 343	5 543
Trade	51 416	56 762	58 480	60 604	64 229	69 579	72 716	74 890	74 523
Transport and communication	22 067	23 862	24 172	25 206	26 163	27 173	29 666	29 980	30 616
Other private sector	152 034	158 490	163 814	168 226	177 962	188 186	200 011	210 922	223 746
less: Imputed bank service charge	–16 819	–17 002	–16 544	–17 450	–18 028	–18 061	–19 769	–20 494	–21 642
Government	47 360	47 880	48 900	48 610	48 800	50 580	52 410	54 930	56 622
Net domestic product at factor cost	340 890	349 620	350 900	363 310	384 860	408 440	428 920	440 140	447 842
Net income from the rest of the world	–40	–680	–1 150	–3 500	–200	–910	–1 170	–1 370	..
National income	340 850	348 940	349 750	359 810	384 660	407 530	427 750	438 770	..

1. Secretariat estimates.
Sources: CBS, *1992 National Accounts* and OECD, *Quarterly National Accounts.*

Table C. **Income and expenditure of households and private non-profit institutions**

Gld. million, current prices

	1985	1986	1987	1988	1989	1990	1991	1992	1993
Compensation of employees	221 707	231 569	239 356	245 738	252 828	267 714	283 938	299 619	307 399
Wages and salaries	177 056	185 330	192 276	198 318	207 248	238 794	252 478	266 509	273 995
Employers and government contributions to social security	44 651	46 240	47 080	47 420	45 580	28 920	31 460	33 110	33 404
Property and other income	48 799	50 056	51 090	52 710	59 120	63 840	66 020	66 640	67 806
Self-employment income	39 839	40 653	41 322	41 544	41 689	43 065	44 790	46 844	47 781
Net property and entrepreneurial income	8 960	9 402	9 768	11 166	17 431	20 775	21 230	19 796	20 026
Transfers received	128 209	131 360	136 320	142 030	147 750	163 490	172 990	185 360	193 824
Transfers from pension funds (A)	16 209	17 430	18 810	20 040	21 060	23 080	24 700	26 840	28 450
Other transfers	112 000	113 930	117 510	121 990	126 690	140 410	148 290	158 520	165 374
Current receipts	398 718	412 992	426 772	440 476	459 725	495 072	522 955	551 622	569 024
Income taxes	40 935	44 423	46 080	50 010	51 830	62 720	73 110	72 280	77 886
Transfers paid	105 387	104 591	109 050	113 930	111 550	110 230	123 270	131 630	136 138
Social security contributions paid	86 965	85 808	90 310	93 950	91 330	87 910	97 480	104 700	108 400
Other current transfers paid	18 422	18 783	18 740	19 980	20 220	22 320	25 790	26 930	27 738
Other transfer payments	1 485	1 915	1 700	1 420	1 580	1 610	1 790	2 550	2 627
Transfers paid to pension funds (B)	16 937	16 868	17 040	18 560	18 640	20 710	24 000	24 380	25 111
Private consumption	252 914	260 240	267 931	271 633	284 470	303 075	322 986	339 511	349 414
Food	42 650	42 830	43 050	43 480	45 150	47 180	48 890	50 970	..
Clothing and footwear	15 300	16 110	16 640	16 170	16 660	18 000	18 850	19 080	..
Rent	29 870	31 550	32 950	34 910	36 880	39 550	42 640	46 260	..
Durables	36 900	39 670	41 670	41 260	42 920	46 770	48 970	50 200	..
Other	128 194	130 080	133 621	135 813	142 860	151 575	163 636	173 001	..
Current disbursements	399 234	409 250	423 066	435 579	447 867	476 045	519 376	543 428	563 440
Net savings (C)	-517	3 741	3 706	4 897	11 858	19 027	3 579	8 194	5 584
Savings ratio	-0.20	1.42	1.36	1.77	4.00	5.91	1.10	2.36	1.57
Net property income from pension funds (D)	31 120	32 850	34 050	35 570	37 390	39 480	42 900	45 530	48 724
Personal saving (C – A + B + D)	31 332	36 029	35 986	38 987	46 828	56 137	45 779	51 264	50 969
Personal saving ratio	11.02	12.16	11.84	12.55	14.13	15.63	12.41	13.12	12.73

Sources: CBS, *1992 National accounts* and OECD Secretariat.

123

Table D. **Industrial production and productivity**

Index 1980 = 100

	1984	1985	1986	1987	1988	1989	1990	1991	1992	1993
Mining and quarrying	86.22	93.65	87.80	90.84	80.70	84.41	82.97	92.64	92.52	93.78
Manufacturing industries	106.51	109.60	112.52	112.88	118.91	123.77	125.76	127.43	127.71	125.84
Basic metals	107.83	109.58	107.20	112.05	122.30	129.07	126.14	127.51	127.97	132.63
Metal products, machinery and equipment	105.09	109.00	109.73	106.91	108.18	114.09	118.64	119.73	119.27	116.55
Food, beverages and tobacco	108.00	105.00	112.00	111.91	114.89	118.48	123.73	126.18	129.50	129.41
Textiles, clothing and leather	93.58	96.00	90.48	86.96	88.32	91.52	95.20	95.20	87.68	89.52
Chemicals	126.52	134.11	141.93	147.75	156.69	164.06	162.83	163.84	165.40	159.03
Electricity, gas and water	104.83	108.82	113.54	109.27	111.45	115.98	113.31	118.81	119.36	118.93
Total industry	101.50	105.67	105.84	106.81	107.08	111.63	116.27	119.59	119.83	118.53
Manufacturing employment and productivity										
Employment (end of quarter)[1]	88.02	89.52	91.52	92.02	92.66	94.45	96.91	96.91	96.24	..
Output per person-year	121.00	122.43	122.94	122.67	128.33	131.05	129.77	131.50	132.71	..

1. Persons.
Source: OECD, Indicators of Industrial Activity.

Table E. **Money and banking**

End of period

	1984	1985	1986	1987	1988	1989	1990	1991	1992	1993
					Gld. million					
Money supply:										
Total primary liquidity	84 992	90 770²	97 212	104 148	111 312²	119 026	123 934²	129 326	135 069	149 643
Notes and coins	27 797	28 604²	29 771	33 287	34 613	36 001	36 473²	36 986	36 991	37 588
Demand deposits	57 195	62 166²	67 441	70 861	76 699²	83 025	87 461²	92 340	98 078	112 055
Secondary liquidity	59 371	67 158²	69 171	187 161²	209 942²	240 695	263 202²	279 950²	299 988	318 803
Claims of money-creating institutions on:										
Private sector	260 318	271 775²	292 281	301 589²	334 478²	400 240	428 930	458 074	465 319	515 509
Central government	56 629	62 462²	65 679	58 857²	62 959	66 603	68 259	67 059	66 274	67 041
Local government	21 108	22 915²	29 532	33 199	33 353²	60 389	59 913	58 680	59 287	62 036
Foreign sector	6 883	9 455	13 961	16 769	23 058	22 439	25 204	25 465	30 016	31 423
					Per cent					
Interest rates:[1]										
Official discount	5.00	5.25	4.58	4.40	3.65	5.92	7.04	7.84	8.31	6.26
Call money (Amsterdam)	5.78	6.30	5.83	5.16	4.45	6.99	8.28	9.00	9.27	7.07
Three-month loans to local authorities	6.10	6.32	5.61	5.31	4.77	7.33	8.62	9.21	9.29	6.75
Capital market yields:[1]										
Government bonds	8.04	7.26	6.31	6.28	6.05	7.24	9.01	8.84	8.18	6.33
of which: Short-term	7.97	7.13	6.15	6.17	5.82	7.26	9.05	8.91	8.22	6.01
Medium-term	8.10	7.32	6.36	6.35	6.16	7.21	8.99	8.79	8.12	6.21
Privately placed public utility loans	8.56	7.79	6.79	6.96	6.83	7.56	9.15	8.90	8.30	6.60
Mortgages on dwellings	8.99	8.36	7.26	7.30	7.12	8.15	9.60	9.80	9.30	7.60

1. Yearly average.
2. Start of new series.
Source: De Nederlandsche Bank, *Annual Report 1993.*

Table F. Merchandise trade
US$ million

	Imports, cif						Exports, fob					
	1987	1988	1989	1990	1991	1992	1987	1988	1989	1990	1991	1992
Total	91 252	99 741	104 216	126 123	125 838	134 375	92 827	103 207	107 803	131 810	133 526	139 918
By areas:												
OECD countries	75 793	81 388	83 691	101 931	102 466	109 313	81 904	86 303	91 681	112 749	114 199	118 537
EC (12)	58 482	63 213	64 600	78 862	79 335	84 577	69 478	73 807	78 398	97 500	99 077	103 012
Other Europe	6 652	6 800	7 248	8 994	8 439	9 293	6 671	6 653	6 985	8 575	8 820	8 737
North America	7 155	7 773	8 374	9 573	9 693	10 116	4 550	4 555	4 817	5 067	4 631	5 020
Japan	3 029	3 159	3 087	3 977	4 552	4 826	724	845	984	1 028	1 151	1 157
Australia	397	368	331	471	395	446	387	366	406	487	438	517
New Zealand	75	73	49	50	51	52	92	74	88	89	79	92
Non-OECD countries	15 451	16 027	17 428	20 823	20 049	21 081	10 135	10 649	10 187	11 472	11 956	13 430
Developed countries[1]	188	210	197	265	221	220	289	311	280	308	377	342
Eastern Europe	2 269	2 052	2 405	2 797	2 149	2 473	1 300	1 409	1 683	1 780	2 116	2 553
China	351	457	495	720	1 029	983	182	257	239	189	238	294
Developing countries	12 641	13 306	14 330	17 040	16 649	17 403	8 364	8 671	7 984	9 193	9 224	10 240
Unspecified	7	2 325	3 096	3 368	3 321	3 980	787	6 254	5 933	7 588	7 370	7 950
By SITC sections:												
0. Food and live animals	10 584	12 284	10 637	12 163	12 911	14 527	17 059	18 669	19 014	22 548	23 070	25 118
1. Beverages and tobacco	1 286	1 294	1 294	1 604	1 743	2 048	2 007	2 003	2 117	2 926	3 171	3 570
2. Crude materials, except fuels	4 921	5 701	6 040	6 648	5 886	6 364	5 378	6 378	6 552	7 453	7 647	8 048
3. Mineral fuels, lubricants, etc.	10 273	9 348	10 871	13 273	12 013	11 594	10 310	8 886	9 879	12 997	13 352	12 151
4. Animal and vegetable oils and fats	495	604	624	627	589	742	683	725	804	854	861	966
5. Chemicals	9 653	10 780	11 490	13 194	13 033	14 393	16 739	19 514	19 394	22 345	21 411	22 061
6. Manufactured goods classified chiefly by material	15 075	17 201	17 887	21 795	21 027	21 854	13 024	15 043	15 896	18 886	18 979	19 383
7. Machinery and transport equipment	26 174	28 974	31 372	38 972	40 002	42 415	19 427	22 930	24 366	30 979	31 427	33 347
8. Other manufactures	12 079	13 006	13 367	17 222	18 150	19 872	7 720	8 608	9 302	12 233	12 998	14 685
9. Other non classified	708	545	628	619	481	563	475	448	475	587	606	585

1. South Africa only.
Source: OECD, Foreign Trade Statistics, Series A and C.

	1980	1985	1987	1988	1989	1990	1991	1992	1993
Budget Indicators: General Government Accounts (%GDP)									
Current receipts	46.3	45.3	48.0	48.2	45.2	44.9	47.4	47.6	48.8
Non-interest expenditures	49.2	47.8	48.4	47.8	46.1	46.6	47.2	48.1	48.6
Primary budget balance	-3.0	-2.4	-0.4	0.5	-0.8	-1.7	0.2	-0.5	0.2
Net interest (including net capital transfers)	-0.9	-1.4	-4.7	-4.6	-3.9	-3.3	-2.7	-2.9	-3.1
General government budget balance	-3.9	-3.9	-5.1	-4.2	-4.7	-5.0	-2.4	-3.5	-2.9
Structure of expenditure and taxation (% GDP)									
Government expenditure	50.4	52.7	53.5	52.8	50.8	51.3	52.1	52.8	53.5
Consumption	17.4	15.7	15.8	15.3	14.8	14.5	14.4	14.5	14.5
Transfers	26.1	26.9	26.9	27.0	26.6	27.7	28.2	29.0	29.7
Subsidies	2.9	3.6	4.4	4.1	3.5	3.0	3.3	3.1	2.9
Investment	3.5	2.8	2.6	2.7	2.6	2.7	2.6	2.7	2.6
Memorandum item:									
Education	..	4.8	4.6	4.4	4.2	4.0	4.0	4.1	..
Total taxes and social security contributions	45.0	44.1	47.5	47.7	44.9	44.6	47.2	46.9	48.1
Tax of individuals	11.8	8.6	9.3	9.8	9.6	11.0	12.3	11.7	12.4
of which: Wage tax	9.6	7.0	7.9	7.9	8.0	9.5	10.6	10.1	10.4
Income tax	1.9	1.2	1.0	1.4	1.1	1.0	1.3	1.1	1.5
Corporate tax	3.0	3.1	3.7	3.5	3.2	3.4	3.4	3.1	3.3
Social security contributions	17.1	19.5	20.2	20.2	18.5	16.7	17.6	18.2	18.5
of which: Employees	7.1	8.7	8.9	8.9	8.3	10.3	10.9	11.5	11.8
Employers	8.0	7.8	8.0	7.8	7.1	3.3	3.5	3.4	3.7
Self-employed or non-employed	2.0	3.0	3.3	3.5	3.1	3.0	3.2	3.3	3.6
Taxes on property	1.6	1.5	1.7	1.7	1.7	1.6	1.7	1.7	1.7
Consumption tax	11.4	11.3	12.4	12.3	11.8	11.8	12.0	12.1	11.9
of which: Value added	7.1	7.1	7.8	7.9	7.3	7.3	7.4	7.2	7.0
Excises	2.4	2.4	2.7	2.6	2.5	2.6	2.6	2.9	3.0
Other taxes	0.1	0.1	0.1	0.1	0.1	0.1	0.2	0.2	0.2
Other indicators									
Income tax elasticity	1.1	-1.0	1.0	2.8	0.8	3.0	3.1	-0.3	2.5
Income tax as % of total tax	32.8	26.3	27.4	27.9	28.5	32.2	33.4	31.4	32.6
Net public debt as a % of GDP	24.5	42.3	51.0	54.0	55.8	56.8	56.3	57.7	59.6

	Until end of 1989	After the 1990 reform[1]	1993
Tax rates			
Income tax			
Top rate	72%	60%	60%
Lower rate	14%	7%[2]	13%[2]
Number of brackets	9	3	3
Average social security tax rate			
Employees	21%	26.85%	28.35%
Employers	19.95%	9.15%	10.25%
VAT rate	6%-20%	6%-18.5%	6%-17.5%
Corporation tax rate	42%	40%-35%[3]	40%-35%

1. Changes mainly due to the "Oort" Reform. The change in the corporation tax rate took place in October 1988 and in the VAT rate in January 1989.
2. This rate is 35 per cent including the social security tax for AOW (pensions), AWW (widows and orphans), AWBZ (health care) and AAW (disablement). For 1993 this rate is 38.4 per cent. People over 65 are exempted from AOW/AWW; their total first bracket tax rate is 18 per cent instead of 35 per cent.
3. 40 per cent for the first Gld 250 000 profit and 35 per cent over that amount.
Sources: CPB, Central Economic Plan 1994; OECD, *National Accounts, Revenue Statistics of OECD Member countries* and Secretariat estimates.

Table H. Structure of output and performance indicators

A. Structure of output (constant prices)

	1986	1987	1988	1989	1990	1991	1992
	Share of GDP						
Agriculture, hunting, forestry and fishing	3.9	3.7	3.8	3.8	4.0	4.0	4.0
Mining and quarrying	3.5	3.6	3.1	3.1	3.0	3.2	3.1
Manufacturing	19.2	18.6	18.9	19.0	19.0	18.7	18.6
of which:							
Food, beverages and tobacco	3.3	2.7	2.7	3.0	3.1	3.1	3.1
Textile and leather industries	0.7	0.6	0.6	0.6	0.6	0.6	0.6
Wood industry	0.5	0.5	0.5	0.5	0.5	0.5	0.5
Paper industry	2.1	2.1	2.2	2.2	2.1	2.1	2.1
Chemicals and rubber industries	4.8	4.7	4.9	4.9	4.9	4.7	4.8
Metal and other products	7.9	7.8	7.8	7.8	7.8	7.7	7.5
Electricity, gas and water	1.8	1.8	1.8	1.7	1.7	1.7	1.7
Construction	5.2	5.2	5.6	5.4	5.2	5.1	5.1
Trade, restaurants and hotels	14.6	14.5	14.5	14.6	14.7	15.0	14.9
Transport, storage and communication	5.9	5.9	6.0	6.1	6.2	6.4	6.5
Other services[1]	29.8	30.2	30.3	30.3	30.2	30.4	30.5
Total business sector	83.8	83.5	83.9	84.0	84.1	84.5	84.5
Government	10.8	10.9	10.7	10.3	10.0	9.8	9.7
	Share of total employment						
Agriculture, hunting, forestry and fishing	5.5	5.3	5.3	5.1	5.0	4.9	4.9
Mining and quarrying	0.2	0.2	0.2	0.2	0.2	0.2	0.2
Manufacturing	18.9	18.8	18.7	18.6	18.5	18.1	17.8
of which:							
Food, beverages and tobacco	3.3	3.2	3.2	3.1	3.1	3.0	3.0
Textile and leather industries	1.0	1.0	1.0	1.0	1.0	1.0	0.9
Wood industry	0.7	0.7	0.8	0.8	0.8	0.8	0.8
Paper industry	2.2	2.2	2.2	2.3	2.2	2.2	2.2
Chemicals and rubber industries	2.6	2.6	2.6	2.6	2.6	2.5	2.5
Metal and other products	9.2	9.1	8.9	8.8	8.8	8.6	8.4
Electricity, gas and water	0.9	0.9	0.9	0.9	0.9	0.8	0.8
Construction	7.5	7.6	7.7	7.6	7.5	7.4	7.2
Trade, restaurants and hotels	18.9	19.1	19.3	19.6	20.0	20.3	20.5
Transport, storage and communication	6.8	6.8	6.7	6.7	6.7	6.8	6.8
Other services[1]	25.5	25.7	25.9	26.3	26.7	27.2	27.7
Total business sector	84.3	84.4	84.7	85.0	85.4	85.7	86.0
Government	14.6	14.5	14.2	13.8	13.5	13.1	12.9
	Share of total investment[2]						
Agriculture, hunting, forestry and fishing	5.2	4.3	4.8	5.1	5.2	5.2	5.0
Mining and quarrying	26.0	25.6	23.1	22.1	22.0	21.5	20.7
Manufacturing	:	:	:	:	:	:	:

B. Economic performance (constant prices)

	1986	1987	1988	1989	1990	1991	1992
	Productivity growth						
Agriculture, hunting, forestry and fishing	..	-3.7	4.4	7.3	9.6	3.0	0.5
Mining and quarrying	..	3.7	-11.9	3.4	1.3	-1.4	-1.4
Manufacturing	..	-2.9	3.4	4.1	1.9	1.1	1.7
of which:							
Food, beverages and tobacco	..	-14.6	2.3	14.4	6.9	1.1	3.7
Textile and leather industries	..	-3.0	-1.6	0.0	0.7	3.5	-1.8
Wood industry	..	2.3	0.3	-0.7	-5.6	0.4	0.8
Paper industry	..	1.4	3.1	0.4	1.6	1.5	-1.5
Chemicals and rubber industries	..	-2.1	5.8	2.0	1.3	-1.0	4.6
Metal and other products	..	-0.5	2.8	4.2	1.3	1.8	0.1
Electricity, gas and water	..	-0.7	2.3	0.2	5.2	7.3	0.7
Construction	..	0.2	6.6	0.3	0.3	-1.1	3.9

	1979	1980	1981	1982	1983	1984	1985	1986	1987	1988	1989	1990	1991	1992
Transport, storage and communication	..	1.2	3.0	3.1	4.2	1.8	1.7	..	..	..	..	..	..	..
Other services[1]	..	0.3	0.2	1.4	-0.1	-0.9	-0.5	40.0	42.1	43.4	43.0	43.2	42.3	43.5
Total business sector	..	-0.9	1.1	2.5	1.4	0.6	0.3	90.4	90.6	90.6	91.1	91.1	69.5	70.0
Government	1.5	0.7	1.7	1.5	1.5	1.5	1.4	11.8	11.9	12.0	11.6	12.3	12.1	12.3

C. Other indicators (current prices)

	1979	1980	1981	1982	1983	1984	1985	1986	1987	1988	1989	1990	1991	1992
R&D as % of GDP in manufacturing sector	5.1	5.3	5.6	5.6	6.0	5.7	6.2	6.6	7.0	6.6	6.3	5.7	5.3	..
Total R&D expenditure as % of total GDP	1.9	1.9	1.9	1.9	2.0	1.9	2.1	2.2	2.3	2.2	2.1	2.0	1.9	..
Government funded R&D as % of total	48.0	47.8	47.2	48.5	47.2	46.8	44.2	44.0	44.3	42.7	41.8	45.1	44.9	..
Breakdown of employed workforce by size of establishment:[3]														
1 to 9 type-workers	80.4	80.7	80.5	80.1	80.6	81.1	82.0	82.4	82.0	81.4	81.4	81.8	81.5	81.5
10 to 99 type-workers	17.6	17.4	17.7	18.1	17.6	17.1	16.3	16.0	16.3	16.8	16.8	16.3	16.6	16.6
Over 100 type-workers	1.9	1.9	1.8	1.8	1.8	1.8	1.7	1.7	1.7	1.8	1.9	1.8	1.8	1.8
Total	100.0	100.0	100.0	100.0	100.0	100.0	100.0	100.0	100.0	100.0	100.0	100.0	100.0	100.0
Workforce (thousands of type-workers)	210.71	214.73	217.47	215.91	215.96	215.72	220.46	223.22	223.29	223.88	233.58	241.81	251.02	263.15

1. Excluding government services.
2. Mining and quarrying also includes manufacturing (including repair services), electricity, gas and water and construction.
3. Entreprises (excl. government) classified by the number of type-workers (1 type-worker = 250 man-days; since 1985, 1 type-worker = 260 man-days).
Sources: CBS, *Statistical Yearbook of the Netherlands 1994*, and, *1992 National Accounts*; OECD, *National Accounts* and *Main Science and Technology Indicators*.

Table I. Labour market indicators

A. Evolution

	Peak	Trough	1988	1989	1990	1991	1992	1993
Registered unemployment rate[1]	1983: 12.0	1970: 1.0	7.7	6.9	5.9	5.4	5.3	6.5
Share of long term unemployment[1,2]	1985: 60.7	1981: 29.6	45.6	50.0	55.3	52.7	49.1	45.3
Beneficiaries as a % of labour force			10.8	10.3	9.5	9.1	9.3	10.3
National unemployment rate[3]								
Total	1984: 14.2	1971: 1.3	8.4	7.6	6.9	6.5	6.5	7.5
Male	1984: 14.6	1979: 3.6	6.1	5.4	4.6	4.6	4.7	5.7
Female	1984: 13.5	1971: 0.9	12.5	11.7	10.9	9.7	9.7	10.5
Youth[4]	1984: 25.2	1971: 1.4	12.5	11.2	10.3	10.0	9.5	11.8
Registered vacancies (thousands)[5]	1990: 115.4	1982: 17.6	92.6	92.6	115.4	98.0	71.0	39.0
Paid hours per job, full-time[6]			1 770	1 770	1 773	1 773	1 773	..
Paid hours per job, total[6]			1 473	1 464	1 457	1 447	1 441	..

B. Structural or institutional characteristics

	1970	1980	1988	1989	1990	1991	1992	1993
Labour force (percentage change)	0.6[10]	0.6[12]	2.2	1.1	2.3	2.1	1.7	1.8
Participation rate:[7]								
Total	..	53.6	58.1	58.3	59.3	60.1	60.8	61.5
Male	..	79.4	74.2	74.3	74.6	75.0	75.6	75.5
Female	..	35.5	41.5	41.9	43.6	44.9	45.7	47.0
Employment/population between 15 and 64 years	57.7	51.3	53.2	53.9	55.2	56.2	56.9	56.9
Civilian employment by sector (percentage change)								
Agriculture	-1.5[11]	0.3[12]	-1.2	1.2	3.6	-1.2	-6.7	-2.5
Industry	-0.7[11]	-1.8[12]	1.4	1.8	2.9	0.1	-1.2	-1.7
Services	2.8[11]	1.5[12]	2.9	1.9	3.1	3.8	3.3	1.8
of which: Government (full-time equivalents)	2.3[11]	0.6[12]	-0.5	-0.5	-0.4	-0.9	-0.8	0.0
Total	1.4[11]	0.4[12]	2.3	1.9	3.1	2.6	1.7	0.7
Civilian employment by sector (% of total)								
Agriculture	5.7[13]	4.9	4.6	4.6	4.6	4.4	4.0	3.9
Industry	34.9[13]	31.5	27.6	27.6	27.6	26.9	26.2	25.6
Services	59.4[13]	63.6	67.8	67.8	67.9	68.7	69.8	70.5
of which: Government (full-time equivalents)	13.6[13]	14.4	13.9	13.6	13.2	12.7	12.4	12.3
Total	100.0	100.0	100.0	100.0	100.0	100.0	100.0	100.0
Part-time employment[8] (per cent of total employees)	17.4	17.6	32.2	32.6	33.2	34.3	32.8	..
Non-wage labour cost[9]	13.6	16.4	16.4	15.6	9.8	10.1	10.1	9.9
Gross minimum wage as a % of average worker wage	72.8[13]	71.0	62.8	62.8	62.4	67.8	63.8	

1. Official registered unemployment rate.
2. People looking for a job since one year or more as a percentage of total unemployment.
3. According to the national definition (CBS, *Labour Market Survey*), people working less than 12 hours per week are not counted as employed.
4. People between 15 and 24 years as a percentage of the labour force of the same age group.
5. Based on survey data, Secretariat estimates for 1988.
6. The sum of contractual hours and overtime per job.
7. Labour force as a percentage of the corresponding population aged between 15 and 64 years.
8. Employees working less than 35 hours per week.
9. Total employers' contributions as a percentage of total compensation.
10. 1970-79 average.
11. 1975-79 average.
12. 1980-84 average.
13. 1975 figure.

Sources: CBS, *Labour Market Survey 1993, Statistical Yearbook of the Netherlands 1994, Monthly Labour Force Survey and Bi-annual Labour Force Survey;* Ministry for Social Affairs and Employment; OECD, *Main Economic Indicators, Labour Force Statistics* and Secretariat estimates.

Table J. **Financial markets**

	1970	1980	1985	1989	1990	1991	1992	1993
A. Sector size								
Sector employment[1]/total employment	2.8	3.6	3.6	3.6	3.5	3.5	3.5	..
Sector GDP[1]/total GDP	3.0	4.7	4.8	5.0	4.6	4.6	4.7	..
Funds redistributed by financial institutions/GDP	..	..	11.1	20.4	18.5	9.7	19.2	22.8
Domestic financial assets of financial sector/GDP	98.2	143.4	195.0	248.1	243.8	242.7	248.0	265.0
Stock-market capitalisation[2]/GDP	..	18.3	38.7	47.1	37.5	41.0	41.6	59.4
B. Structure of financial flows								
Share of domestic intermediated finance in external financing of non-financial enterprises[3]	..	23.2	..	34.7	30.2	42.6	40.0	30.2
Securities issues in domestic credit flows[4]		21.8	41.2	42.7	52.7	57.8	60.7	51.7
Structure of non-financial corporate liabilities:[5]								
Equity	..	..	34.5	37.5	37.3	37.1	36.9	..
Short-term: interest bearing	..	..	7.7	7.4	7.0	7.9	8.5	..
non-interest bearing	..	..	28.0	25.1	24.9	24.1	23.3	..
Long-term: interest bearing	..	..	20.0	21.7	22.8	23.3	23.7	..
non-interest bearing	..	..	9.7	8.3	8.0	7.5	7.7	..
C. Internationalisation of markets								
Foreign business of the banking sector:[6]								
Assets	25.8	34.2	33.6	31.2	32.4	32.6	32.8	33.5
Liabilities	24.7	35.4	29.8	25.8	26.7	27.1	28.5	29.0
International banking networks:								
Foreign banking presence[7]	..	23	42	43	47	46	48	50
Foreign claims in % of domestic assets	25.7	33.7	30.7	26.6	27.4	27.0	27.4	28.2
Relative size of cross-border transactions in securities:[8]								
Net purchases of foreign securities by domestic residents	..	1.9	-22.0	-2.4	-14.3	-17.6	-39.0	-25.8
Net purchases of domestic securities by foreign residents	..	34.5	25.9	35.4	-6.3	13.9	12.1	34.6
D. Efficiency of markets								
Interest rate margins[9]	2.6	2.6	2.5	1.8	1.7	1.8	1.8	..
Banks' productivity[10]	73.8	84.0	75.0	65.6	68.5	68.1	67.8	..

Three-month loans to local authorities/Euro-Guilder three-month

deposit rate	..	..	-0.05	-0.03	-0.02	-0.04	-0.03	-0.03
Money market: Netherlands-Germany	..	..	1.07	0.34	0.20	0.07	-0.08	-0.40
Netherlands-United States	..	..	-1.96	-1.85	0.44	3.37	5.59	3.55
Capital market: Netherlands-Germany	..	..	0.29	0.28	0.22	0.29	0.33	-0.08
Netherlands-United States	-7.35	-11.44	-3.28	-1.29	0.37	0.88	1.10	0.48

1. Sector defined as financial institutions (including insurance sector).
2. Excluding investment funds.
3. External financing is the sum of intermediated financing (by financial institutions) and non-intermediated financing (share or bond financing, direct foreign investment in the Netherlands and direct borrowing abroad).
4. Value of net bond and share issues by residents as percentage of change in total long-term credit borrowed by residents.
5. The non-financial sector is represented by manufacturing industries, trade corporations, transport corporations and services corporations.
6. Money-creating institutions excluding Nederlandsche Bank; as percentage of balance sheet total.
7. Number of branches and subsidiaries.
8. Ratio of cross-border transactions in securities to issues by residents.
9. Interest received minus interest paid divided by total assets.
10. Expenses divided by earnings of universal banks, Rabobanks and, as from 1986, the Postbank. As from 1990 all registered institutions.
11. Net pre-tax earnings as percentage of balance sheet total of universal banks, Rabobanks and, as from 1986, the Postbank. As from 1990 all registered institutions.
12. Differential between Euro-currency 3-month deposit rates (money market) and Government bonds (capital market); yearly averages.

Source: De Nederlandsche Bank, *Quarterly Bulletin 1993/4,* and *Annual Report 1993.*

BASIC STATISTICS

BASIC STATISTICS:

INTERNATIONAL COMPARISONS

	Units	Reference period [1]	Australia	Austr
Population				
Total	Thousands	1991	17 292	7 823
Inhabitants per sq. km	Number	1991	2	93
Net average annual increase over previous 10 years	%	1991	1.5	0.3
Employment				
Total civilian employment (TCE) [2]	Thousands	1991	7 705	3 482
Of which: Agriculture	% of TCE		5.5	7.4
Industry	% of TCE		24.2	36.9
Services	% of TCE		70.4	55.8
Gross domestic product (GDP)				
At current prices and current exchange rates	Bill. US$	1991	297.4	164.7
Per capita	US$		17 200	21 048
At current prices using current PPP's [3]	Bill. US$	1991	280	135.6
Per capita	US$		16 195	17 329
Average annual volume growth over previous 5 years	%	1991	2.8	3.3
Gross fixed capital formation (GFCF)	% of GDP	1991	20.5	25.1
Of which: Machinery and equipment	% of GDP		8.8	10.4
Residential construction	% of GDP		4.6	4.6
Average annual volume growth over previous 5 years	%	1991	0.3	5.2
Gross saving ratio [4]	% of GDP	1991	17.2	25.6
General government				
Current expenditure on goods and services	% of GDP	1991	18.3	18.2
Current disbursements [5]	% of GDP	1991	36.6	45.7
Current receipts	% of GDP	1991	33.7	47.2
Net official development assistance	% of GDP	1991	0.35	0.33
Indicators of living standards				
Private consumption per capita using current PPP's [3]	US$	1991	9 827	9 591
Passenger cars, per 1 000 inhabitants	Number	1990	430	382
Telephones, per 1 000 inhabitants	Number	1990	448 (89)	589
Television sets, per 1 000 inhabitants	Number	1989	484	475
Doctors, per 1 000 inhabitants	Number	1991	2	2.1
Infant mortality per 1 000 live births	Number	1991	7.1	7.4
Wages and prices (average annual increase over previous 5 years)				
Wages (earnings or rates according to availability)	%	1991	5.4	5.2
Consumer prices	%	1991	6.7	2.5
Foreign trade				
Exports of goods, fob*	Mill. US$	1991	39 764	40 985
As % of GDP	%		13.4	24.9
Average annual increase over previous 5 years	%		13.2	12.8
Imports of goods, cif*	Mill. US$	1991	38 844	48 914
As % of GDP	%		13.1	29.7
Average annual increase over previous 5 years	%		10.1	13.7
Total official reserves [6]	Mill. SDR's	1991	11 432	6 591
As ratio of average monthly imports of goods	Ratio		3.5	1.6

* At current prices and exchange rates.
1. Unless otherwise stated.
2. According to the definitions used in OECD *Labour Force Statistics*.
3. PPP's = Purchasing Power Parities.
4. Gross saving = Gross national disposable income minus private and government consumption.
5. Current disbursements = Current expenditure on goods and services plus current transfers and payments of property income.
6. Gold included in reserves is valued at 35 SDR's per ounce. End of year.
7. Including Luxembourg.

Belgium	Canada	Denmark	Finland	France	Germany	Greece	Iceland	Ireland
0 005	27 000	5 154	5 029	57 050	63 889	10 269	258	3 524
328	3	120	15	104	257	78	3	50
0.2	1	0.1	0.5	0.5	0.4	0.5	1.1	0.2
3 735	12 340	2 612	2 330	21 782	28 533	3 768	140	1 113
2.6	4.5	5.7	8.5	5.8	3.4	22.6	10.7	13.8
28.1	23.2	27.7	29.2	29.5	39.2	27.5	26.4	28.9
69.3	72.3	66.6	62.3	64.8	57.4	50	62.9	57.2
196.9	583.7	130.3	121.2	1 195.8	1 587.8	70.2	6.5	43.4
9 677	21 617	25 277	24 097	20 961	24 852	6 840	25 232	12 324
171.5	520.6	90.7	77.8	1 035.6	1 257.8	79.4	4.5	40.5
7 145	19 281	17 603	15 480	18 152	19 687	7 729	17 442	11 480
3.2	1.9	1.1	1.4	2.7	3.8	1.9	2	5.4
19.8	20	16.9	22.4	20.9	21.4	18.6	18.9	17.1
10.4 (90)	6.4	8.5	7.4	9.4	10	7.8	6	7.7
4.2	6.2	3.2	6.1	5.1	5.7	4.4	4.1	4.1
8.5	4.2	-2.9	0.1	4.6	5.4	3.5	2.6	3
21.4	14.4	17.9	14.7	20.7	23.1	15.3	14.4	23.7
14.7	21.3	25.1	24.4	18.3	17.7	19.9	20	16.3
54.6	47.9	57.2	46	47	44.2	47.6	32.5	49.9 (8
49.8	43.1	55.5	42.6	46.5	44.5	37	35.1	43.7 (8
0.42	0.45	0.92	0.77	0.62	0.43	0.08	0.12	0.17
0 756	11 634	9 139	8 686	10 928	10 672	5 516	10 731	6 409
387	469	311	386	413	480	169	464	228
546	570	972	530	482	671	458	496	279
447	626	528	488	400	506	195	319	271
3.6	2.2	2.8	2.5	2.7	3.2	3.4	2.8	1.5
8.4	6.8	7.5	5.8	7.3	7.1	9	5.5	8.2
3.5	4.5	5.9	8.3	3.8	4.7	16.9	. .	5.3
2.5	4.8	3.7	5.2	3.2	2.1	16.7	17.2	3.2
3 291 [7]	127 658	34 988	26 508	216 157	409 620	8 014	1 589	23 796
60.1	21.9	26.9	21.9	18.1	25.8	11.4	24.4	54.8
11.4	7.9	11.1	7.1	11.7	10.6	8.9	8.1	14
0 330 [7]	116 729	31 647	26 953	225 260	344 454	19 831	1 655	20 687
61.1	20	24.3	22.2	18.8	21.7	28.2	25.4	47.6
12	7.8	7.2	7.2	12.2	15.3	11.9	9	12.4
3 541 [7]	12 544	7 445	6 779	25 851	47 729	2 398	307	3 672
0.9	1.3	2.8	3	1.4	1.7	1.5	2.2	2.1

8. Included in B
9. Including nor
Sources: Populat
GDP, GFCF,
Indicators of
Wages and pr
Foreign trade
Total official

	Italy	Japan	Luxembourg	Netherlands	New Zealand	Norway	Po
	57 114	123 920	390	15 070	3 406	4 262	9 8
	190	328	150	369	13	13	3
	0.1	0.5	0.6	0.6	0.8	0.4	
	21 410	63 690	162	6 444	1 451	1 973	4 6
	8.5	6.7	3.7	4.5	10.8	5.9	1
	32.3	34.4	31.5	25.5	23.5	23.7	3
	59.2	58.9	64.8	69.9	65.7	70.4	4
	1 149.9	3 346.4	9.3	289.8	42.2	105.9	6
	19 900	27 005	24 186	19 232	12 400	24 853	6 9
	974.6	2 349.2	8.1	248	46.6	71.6	9
	16 866	18 957	20 904	16 453	13 675	16 804	9 1
	2.7	4.8	4.3	2.9	-0.2	1.1	
	19.8	31.7	29	20.5	16.4	18.5	
	9.4	13.1	12.4	10	9.9 (90)	11.7 (87)	
	5.3	5.5	5.5	4.7	4.8 (90)	2.1	
	4.1	8.5	9.9	2.5	-1.3	-6.6	
	18.6	35.1	59.4	24.7	15	23.6	2
	17.5	9.2	17.1	14.4	16.6	21.5	1
")	49.4	25.4	45 (86)	54.8	..	52.9	3
)	43	34.4	52.9 (86)	54.6	..	55.3	3
	0.29	0.33	0.42	0.87	0.24	1.1	0.
	10 418	10 738	11 973	9 807	8 771	8 558	5 8
	478	282	470	356 (89)	440	378	2
	555	421	413	462	430	502	2
	423	610	252	485	372	423	1
	1.3	1.6	2.1	2.5	1.9	3.1	2
	8.3	4.6	9.2	6.5	8.3	7	10
	7.1	4.1		2.2	5.2	7.6	
	5.7	1.9	2.3	1.5	7.2	5.5	11
	170 258	286 314	8	131 361	9 515	33 808	16 3.
	14.8	8.6	..	45.3	22.5	31.9	23
	11.6	8.5	..	10.6	10.5	13.1	17
	181 925	233 814	..	126 158	9 464	27 164	24 8
	15.8	7	..	43.5	22.4	25.6	36
	12.8	13.1	..	10.9	6.8	4.6	22
	44 232	55 179	..	12 289	2 902	10 777	10 18
	2.9	2.8	..	1.2	3.7	4.8	4

lgium.
residential construction.
on and employment: OECD, *Labour Force Statistics*.
nd general government: OECD, *National Accounts*, Vol. 1 and *OECD Economic Outlook*, Historical Statistics.
ving standards: miscellaneous national publications.
es: OECD, *Main Economic Indicators*.
OECD, *Monthly Foreign Trade Statistics*, series A.
serves: IMF, *International Financial Statistics*.

	Spain	Sweden	Switzerland	Turkey	United Kingdom	United States
	39 025	8 617	6 792	57 693	57 649	252 160
	77	19	165	74	236	27
	0.3	0.3	0.6	2.3	0.2	0.9
	12 608	4 431	3 560	18 171	25 726	116 877
	10.7	3.2	5.5	46.6	2.2	2.9
	33.1	28.2	34.4	20.3	27.8	25.3
	56.3	68.5	60.1	33.1	70	71.8
	527.6	239.3	230.9	108	1 008.4	5 610.8
	13 519	27 774	33 992	1 872	17 492	22 204
	496.2	145.4	148.3	201.1	899.8	5 610.8
	12 714	16 877	21 832	3 486	15 608	22 204
	4.3	1.6	2.2	4.7	2	1.9
	23.9	19.4	25.6	22.8	16.9	15.4
	7.1					
(90)	4.7	6.2	16.9⁹	5.8 (87)	3	3.4
	9.9	3.3	4	3.1	2.8	−0.5
	21	16	31.6	21.2	13.5	15
	16.1	27.2	13.9	22.5	21.7	18.2
(90)	35.5 (88)	59.8	32.5	..	39.7	36.7
(90)	36.3 (88)	60	34.2	..	38.8	32.5
	0.22	0.88	0.37	..	0.32	0.2
	7 935	8 994	12 607	1995	9 912	14 891
	307	418	441	29	361	568
	323	681	905	151	434	509
	389	471	406	174	434	814
	3.9	2.9	3	0.9	1.4	2.3
	7.8	6.1	6.2	56.5	7.4	8.9
	7.6	7.7	..	..	8.6	2.8
	5.9	7.2	3.5	60.3	6.4	4.4
	55 353	57 422	63 893	13 057	184 087	393 812
	10.5	24	27.7	12.1	18.3	7
	17.1	8.1	10.2	12.9	11.5	13.2
	87 449	54 659	69 863	22 566	222 522	494 842
	16.6	22.8	30.3	20.9	22.1	8.8
	21.6	8.8	10	13.5	10.7	6
	36 008	12 644	20 541	4 252	25 201	50 791
	4.9	2.8	3.5	2.3	1.4	1.2

EMPLOYMENT OPPORTUNITIES

Economics Department, OECD

The Economics Department of the OECD offers challenging and rewarding opportunities to economists interested in applied policy analysis in an international environment. The Department's concerns extend across the entire field of economic policy analysis, both macro-economic and micro-economic. Its main task is to provide, for discussion by committees of senior officials from Member countries, documents and papers dealing with current policy concerns. Within this programme of work, three major responsibilities are:

- to prepare regular surveys of the economies of individual Member countries;
- to issue full twice-yearly reviews of the economic situation and prospects of the OECD countries in the context of world economic trends;
- to analyse specific policy issues in a medium-term context for theOECD as a whole, and to a lesser extent for the non-OECD countries.

The documents prepared for these purposes, together with much of the Department's other economic work, appear in published form in the *OECD Economic Outlook, OECD Economic Surveys, OECD Economic Studies* and the Department's *Working Papers* series.

The Department maintains a world econometric model, INTERLINK, which plays an important role in the preparation of the policy analyses and twice-yearly projections. The availability of extensive cross-country data bases and good computer resources facilitates comparative empirical analysis, much of which is incorporated into the model.

The Department is made up of about 75 professional economists from a variety of backgrounds and Member countries. Most projects are carried out by small teams and last from four to eighteen months. Within the Department, ideas and points of view are widely discussed; there is a lively professional interchange, and all professional staff have the opportunity to contribute actively to the programme of work.

Skills the Economics Department is looking for:

a) Solid competence in using the tools of both micro-economic and macro-economic theory to answer policy questions. Experience indicates that this normally requires the equivalent of a PH.D. in economics or substantial relevant professional experience to compensate for a lower degree.

b) Solid knowledge of economic statistics and quantitative methods; this includes how to identify data, estimate structural relationships, apply basic techniques of time series analysis, and test hypotheses. It is essential to be able to interpret results sensibly in an economic policy context.

c) A keen interest in and knowledge of policy issues, economic developments and their political/social contexts.
d) Interest and experience in analysing questions posed by policy-makers and presenting the results to them effectively and judiciously. Thus, work experience in government agencies or policy research institutions is an advantage.
e) The ability to write clearly, effectively, and to the point. The OECD is a bilingual organisation with French and English as the official languages. Candidates must have excellent knowledge of one of these languages, and some knowledge of the other. Knowledge of other languages might also be an advantage for certain posts.
f) For some posts, expertise in a particular area may be important, but a successful candidate is expected to be able to work on a broader range of topics relevant to the work of the Department. Thus, except in rare cases, the Department does not recruit narrow specialists.
g) The Department works on a tight time schedule and strict deadlines. Moreover, much of the work in the Department is carried out in small groups of economists. Thus, the ability to work with other economists from a variety of cultural and professional backgrounds, to supervise junior staff, and to produce work on time is important.

General Information

The salary for recruits depends on educational and professional background. Positions carry a basic salary from FF 262 512 or FF 323 916 for Administrators (economists) and from FF 375 708 for Principal Administrators (senior economists). This may be supplemented by expatriation and/or family allowances, depending on nationality, residence and family situation. Initial appointments are for a fixed term of two to three years.

Vacancies are open to candidates from OECD Member countries. The Organisation seeks to maintain an appropriate balance between female and male staff and among nationals from Member countries.

For further information on employment opportunities in the Economics Department, contact:

Administrative Unit
Economics Department
OECD
2, rue André-Pascal
75775 PARIS CEDEX 16
FRANCE

Applications citing "ECSUR", together with a detailed *curriculum vitae* in English or French, should be sent to the Head of Personnel at the above address.

MAIN SALES OUTLETS OF OECD PUBLICATIONS
PRINCIPAUX POINTS DE VENTE DES PUBLICATIONS DE L'OCDE

ARGENTINA – ARGENTINE
Carlos Hirsch S.R.L.
Galería Güemes, Florida 165, 4° Piso
1333 Buenos Aires   Tel. (1) 331.1787 y 331.2391
Telefax: (1) 331.1787

AUSTRALIA – AUSTRALIE
D.A. Information Services
648 Whitehorse Road, P.O.B 163
Mitcham, Victoria 3132   Tel. (03) 873.4411
Telefax: (03) 873.5679

AUSTRIA – AUTRICHE
Gerold & Co.
Graben 31
Wien I   Tel. (0222) 533.50.14

BELGIUM – BELGIQUE
Jean De Lannoy
Avenue du Roi 202
B-1060 Bruxelles   Tel. (02) 538.51.69/538.08.41
Telefax: (02) 538.08.41

CANADA
Renouf Publishing Company Ltd.
1294 Algoma Road
Ottawa, ON K1B 3W8   Tel. (613) 741.4333
Telefax: (613) 741.5439
Stores:
61 Sparks Street
Ottawa, ON K1P 5R1   Tel. (613) 238.8985
211 Yonge Street
Toronto, ON M5B 1M4   Tel. (416) 363.3171
Telefax: (416)363.59.63

Les Éditions La Liberté Inc.
3020 Chemin Sainte-Foy
Sainte-Foy, PQ G1X 3V6   Tel. (418) 658.3763
Telefax: (418) 658.3763

Federal Publications Inc.
165 University Avenue, Suite 701
Toronto, ON M5H 3B8   Tel. (416) 860.1611
Telefax: (416) 860.1608

Les Publications Fédérales
1185 Université
Montréal, QC H3B 3A7   Tel. (514) 954.1633
Telefax : (514) 954.1635

CHINA – CHINE
China National Publications Import
Export Corporation (CNPIEC)
16 Gongti E. Road, Chaoyang District
P.O. Box 88 or 50
Beijing 100704 PR   Tel. (01) 506.6688
Telefax: (01) 506.3101

DENMARK – DANEMARK
Munksgaard Book and Subscription Service
35, Nørre Søgade, P.O. Box 2148
DK-1016 København K   Tel. (33) 12.85.70
Telefax: (33) 12.93.87

FINLAND – FINLANDE
Akateeminen Kirjakauppa
Keskuskatu 1, P.O. Box 128
00100 Helsinki
Subscription Services/Agence d'abonnements :
P.O. Box 23
00371 Helsinki   Tel. (358 0) 12141
Telefax: (358 0) 121.4450

FRANCE
OECD/OCDE
Mail Orders/Commandes par correspondance:
2, rue André-Pascal
75775 Paris Cedex 16   Tel. (33-1) 45.24.82.00
Telefax: (33-1) 49.10.42.76
Telex: 640048 OCDE

OECD Bookshop/Librairie de l'OCDE :
33, rue Octave-Feuillet
75016 Paris   Tel. (33-1) 45.24.81.67
(33-1) 45.24.81.81
Documentation Française
29, quai Voltaire
75007 Paris   Tel. 40.15.70.00
Gibert Jeune (Droit-Économie)
6, place Saint-Michel
75006 Paris   Tel. 43.25.91.19
Librairie du Commerce International
10, avenue d'Iéna
75016 Paris   Tel. 40.73.34.60
Librairie Dunod
Université Paris-Dauphine
Place du Maréchal de Lattre de Tassigny
75016 Paris   Tel. (1) 44.05.40.13
Librairie Lavoisier
11, rue Lavoisier
75008 Paris   Tel. 42.65.39.95
Librairie L.G.D.J. - Montchrestien
20, rue Soufflot
75005 Paris   Tel. 46.33.89.85
Librairie des Sciences Politiques
30, rue Saint-Guillaume
75007 Paris   Tel. 45.48.36.02
P.U.F.
49, boulevard Saint-Michel
75005 Paris   Tel. 43.25.83.40
Librairie de l'Université
12a, rue Nazareth
13100 Aix-en-Provence   Tel. (16) 42.26.18.08
Documentation Française
165, rue Garibaldi
69003 Lyon   Tel. (16) 78.63.32.23
Librairie Decitre
29, place Bellecour
69002 Lyon   Tel. (16) 72.40.54.54

GERMANY – ALLEMAGNE
OECD Publications and Information Centre
August-Bebel-Allee 6
D-53175 Bonn   Tel. (0228) 959.120
Telefax: (0228) 959.12.17

GREECE – GRÈCE
Librairie Kauffmann
Mavrokordatou 9
106 78 Athens   Tel. (01) 32.55.321
Telefax: (01) 36.33.967

HONG-KONG
Swindon Book Co. Ltd.
13–15 Lock Road
Kowloon, Hong Kong   Tel. 366.80.31
Telefax: 739.49.75

HUNGARY – HONGRIE
Euro Info Service
Margitsziget, Európa Ház
1138 Budapest   Tel. (1) 111.62.16
Telefax : (1) 111.60.61

ICELAND – ISLANDE
Mál Mog Menning
Laugavegi 18, Pósthólf 392
121 Reykjavik   Tel. 162.35.23

INDIA – INDE
Oxford Book and Stationery Co.
Scindia House
New Delhi 110001   Tel.(11) 331.5896/5308
Telefax: (11) 332.5993
17 Park Street
Calcutta 700016   Tel. 240832

INDONESIA – INDONÉSIE
Pdii-Lipi
P.O. Box 269/JKSMG/88
Jakarta 12790   Tel. 583467
Telex: 62 875

IRELAND – IRLANDE
TDC Publishers – Library Suppliers
12 North Frederick Street
Dublin 1   Tel. (01) 874.48.35
Telefax: (01) 874.84.16

ISRAEL
Praedicta
5 Shatner Street
P.O. Box 34030
Jerusalem 91430   Tel. (2) 52.84.90/1/2
Telefax: (2) 52.84.93

ITALY – ITALIE
Libreria Commissionaria Sansoni
Via Duca di Calabria 1/1
50125 Firenze   Tel. (055) 64.54.15
Telefax: (055) 64.12.57
Via Bartolini 29
20155 Milano   Tel. (02) 36.50.83
Editrice e Libreria Herder
Piazza Montecitorio 120
00186 Roma   Tel. 679.46.28
Telefax: 678.47.51
Libreria Hoepli
Via Hoepli 5
20121 Milano   Tel. (02) 86.54.46
Telefax: (02) 805.28.86
Libreria Scientifica
Dott. Lucio de Biasio 'Aeiou'
Via Coronelli, 6
20146 Milano   Tel. (02) 48.95.45.52
Telefax: (02) 48.95.45.48

JAPAN – JAPON
OECD Publications and Information Centre
Landic Akasaka Building
2-3-4 Akasaka, Minato-ku
Tokyo 107   Tel. (81.3) 3586.2016
Telefax: (81.3) 3584.7929

KOREA – CORÉE
Kyobo Book Centre Co. Ltd.
P.O. Box 1658, Kwang Hwa Moon
Seoul   Tel. 730.78.91
Telefax: 735.00.30

MALAYSIA – MALAISIE
Co-operative Bookshop Ltd.
University of Malaya
P.O. Box 1127, Jalan Pantai Baru
59700 Kuala Lumpur
Malaysia   Tel. 756.5000/756.5425
Telefax: 757.3661

MEXICO – MEXIQUE
Revistas y Periodicos Internacionales S.A. de C.V.
Florencia 57 - 1004
Mexico, D.F. 06600   Tel. 207.81.00
Telefax : 208.39.79

NETHERLANDS – PAYS-BAS
SDU Uitgeverij Plantijnstraat
Externe Fondsen
Postbus 20014
2500 EA's-Gravenhage   Tel. (070) 37.89.880
Voor bestellingen: Telefax: (070) 34.75.778

NEW ZEALAND
NOUVELLE-ZÉLANDE
Legislation Services
P.O. Box 12418
Thorndon, Wellington   Tel. (04) 496.5652
Telefax: (04) 496.5698

NORWAY – NORVÈGE
Narvesen Info Center – NIC
Bertrand Narvesens vei 2
P.O. Box 6125 Etterstad
0602 Oslo 6   Tel. (022) 57.33.00
                                   Telefax: (022) 68.19.01

PAKISTAN
Mirza Book Agency
65 Shahrah Quaid-E-Azam
Lahore 54000   Tel. (42) 353.601
                                   Telefax: (42) 231.730

PHILIPPINE – PHILIPPINES
International Book Center
5th Floor, Filipinas Life Bldg.
Ayala Avenue
Metro Manila   Tel. 81.96.76
                                   Telex 23312 RHP PH

PORTUGAL
Livraria Portugal
Rua do Carmo 70-74
Apart. 2681
1200 Lisboa   Tel.: (01) 347.49.82/5
                                   Telefax: (01) 347.02.64

SINGAPORE – SINGAPOUR
Gower Asia Pacific Pte Ltd.
Golden Wheel Building
41, Kallang Pudding Road, No. 04-03
Singapore 1334   Tel. 741.5166
                                   Telefax: 742.9356

SPAIN – ESPAGNE
Mundi-Prensa Libros S.A.
Castelló 37, Apartado 1223
Madrid 28001   Tel. (91) 431.33.99
                                   Telefax: (91) 575.39.98

Libreria Internacional AEDOS
Consejo de Ciento 391
08009 – Barcelona   Tel. (93) 488.30.09
                                   Telefax: (93) 487.76.59

Llibreria de la Generalitat
Palau Moja
Rambla dels Estudis, 118
08002 – Barcelona
              (Subscripcions) Tel. (93) 318.80.12
              (Publicacions) Tel. (93) 302.67.23
                             Telefax: (93) 412.18.54

SRI LANKA
Centre for Policy Research
c/o Colombo Agencies Ltd.
No. 300-304, Galle Road
Colombo 3   Tel. (1) 574240, 573551-2
                   Telefax: (1) 575394, 510711

SWEDEN – SUÈDE
Fritzes Information Center
Box 16356
Regeringsgatan 12
106 47 Stockholm   Tel. (08) 690.90.90
                                   Telefax: (08) 20.50.21

Subscription Agency/Agence d'abonnements :
Wennergren-Williams Info AB
P.O. Box 1305
171 25 Solna   Tel. (08) 705.97.50
                                   Téléfax : (08) 27.00.71

SWITZERLAND – SUISSE
Maditec S.A. (Books and Periodicals - Livres
et périodiques)
Chemin des Palettes 4
Case postale 266
1020 Renens   Tel. (021) 635.08.65
                                   Telefax: (021) 635.07.80

Librairie Payot S.A.
4, place Pépinet
CP 3212
1002 Lausanne   Tel. (021) 341.33.48
                                   Telefax: (021) 341.33.45

Librairie Unilivres
6, rue de Candolle
1205 Genève   Tel. (022) 320.26.23
                                   Telefax: (022) 329.73.18

Subscription Agency/Agence d'abonnements :
Dynapresse Marketing S.A.
38 avenue Vibert
1227 Carouge   Tel.: (022) 308.07.89
                                   Telefax : (022) 308.07.99

See also – Voir aussi :
OECD Publications and Information Centre
August-Bebel-Allee 6
D-53175 Bonn (Germany)   Tel. (0228) 959.120
                          Telefax: (0228) 959.12.17

TAIWAN – FORMOSE
Good Faith Worldwide Int'l. Co. Ltd.
9th Floor, No. 118, Sec. 2
Chung Hsiao E. Road
Taipei   Tel. (02) 391.7396/391.7397
                    Telefax: (02) 394.9176

THAILAND – THAÏLANDE
Suksit Siam Co. Ltd.
113, 115 Fuang Nakhon Rd.
Opp. Wat Rajbopith
Bangkok 10200   Tel. (662) 225.9531/2
                        Telefax: (662) 222.5188

TURKEY – TURQUIE
Kültür Yayinlari Is-Türk Ltd. Sti.
Atatürk Bulvari No. 191/Kat 13
Kavaklidere/Ankara   Tel. 428.11.40 Ext. 2458
Dolmabahce Cad. No. 29
Besiktas/Istanbul   Tel. 260.71.88
                                   Telex: 43482B

UNITED KINGDOM – ROYAUME-UNI
HMSO
Gen. enquiries   Tel. (071) 873 0011
Postal orders only:
P.O. Box 276, London SW8 5DT
Personal Callers HMSO Bookshop
49 High Holborn, London WC1V 6HB
                                   Telefax: (071) 873 8200
Branches at: Belfast, Birmingham, Bristol, Edin-
burgh, Manchester

UNITED STATES – ÉTATS-UNIS
OECD Publications and Information Centre
2001 L Street N.W., Suite 700
Washington, D.C. 20036-4910 Tel. (202) 785.6323
                            Telefax: (202) 785.0350

VENEZUELA
Libreria del Este
Avda F. Miranda 52, Aptdo. 60337
Edificio Galipán
Caracas 106   Tel. 951.1705/951.2307/951.1297
                        Telegram: Libreste Caracas

Subscription to OECD periodicals may also be
placed through main subscription agencies.

Les abonnements aux publications périodiques de
l'OCDE peuvent être souscrits auprès des
principales agences d'abonnement.

Orders and inquiries from countries where Distribu-
tors have not yet been appointed should be sent to:
OECD Publications Service, 2 rue André-Pascal,
75775 Paris Cedex 16, France.

Les commandes provenant de pays où l'OCDE n'a
pas encore désigné de distributeur devraient être
adressées à : OCDE, Service des Publications,
2, rue André-Pascal, 75775 Paris Cedex 16, France.

                                            6-1994

PRINTED IN FRANCE

•

OECD PUBLICATIONS
2 rue André-Pascal
75775 PARIS CEDEX 16
No. 47399
(10 94 21 1) ISBN 92-64-14216-9
ISSN 0376-6438

•